2 75

DAVID HUME
A Symposium

DAVID HUME

A Symposium

BY

STUART HAMPSHIRE   D. F. PEARS
P. L. GARDINER   G. J. WARNOCK
PHILIPPA FOOT   B. A. O. WILLIAMS
H. R. TREVOR-ROPER

EDITED BY

D. F. PEARS

LONDON
MACMILLAN & CO LTD
NEW YORK · ST MARTIN'S PRESS
1963

MACMILLAN AND COMPANY LIMITED
St Martin's Street London WC 2
also Bombay Calcutta Madras Melbourne

THE MACMILLAN COMPANY OF CANADA LIMITED
Toronto

ST MARTIN'S PRESS INC
New York

PRINTED IN GREAT BRITAIN

CONTENTS

*Most of the essays in this book originated
as talks in the Third Programme
of the B.B.C.*

1

HUME'S PLACE IN PHILOSOPHY

THE place that Hume occupies in the thought of our time offers a paradox, and is not easily understood. At no previous period in the history of philosophy has there been such insistence as there is now on exact argument, on consistency in the use of words, on formal rigour as the only guarantees of truth in abstract argument. Philosophy — it is now generally believed — is essentially argument, and there is an ethics of argument: one must test one's sentences, word by word, rather as a lawyer would in drafting a document, to see that they are clear, consistent, immune to objections, correctly used. Hume's philosophical prose in no way conforms to these requirements, not even in the *Treatise*, and certainly not in the *Enquiries* or in the *Dialogues concerning Natural Religion*; and it was not intended to conform to these standards. On the contrary, his philosophical style was designed to persuade, rather than to prove. And the ethics of persuasion are quite different from the ethics of probative argument. Yet he is still a dominating influence in contemporary philosophy in Britain.

Suppose a man who has arrived, in some moment or moments of enlightenment, at a general view of the sources and limits of human knowledge, a view which at the same time explains why these sources and limits have hitherto been misconceived. He suddenly sees clearly why his predecessors have been so confused and muddled, so inconclusive in their search for philosophical truth. They have overlooked a central distinction, which, once noticed, must be altogether evident. It has been overlooked just because it is so evident, so unlike the sophisticated, elaborate, scholastic distinctions that are ordinarily of concern to philosophers. So the problem of philosophical style is to induce men to look in the right direction, to lead them back from the farfetched distinctions of the learned to the most obvious, most general facts of their experience. Under these conditions it will be in place to use arguments, to cite analogies and examples, which would be inept, and even shocking, in an argument that claims to be some kind of proof. The very same analogies and examples may be altogether apt if they, in fact, make the reader notice what he has overlooked, the simple truth that will be evident to him, as soon as he has been shocked into seeing it.

Hume did in fact have a moment of enlightenment, a kind of conversion, early in his life, when he was twenty-two. We know very little about it, except that it accompanied his recovery from a sense of purposelessness, from *accidie*, from a crisis in his mental life. This crisis he reports in a famous letter. When he came to write the *Treatise of Human Nature*, very soon afterwards, his philosophical vision was already fully formed and clear. It never subsequently changed. His outlook upon human experience, on the proper limits of knowledge, on the nature of the sentiments and of society, on the relation between thought and conduct, remained stable, and nothing was to disturb it. His later writing was exposition, neither itself the process of discovery, nor the record of it. The difference between the *Treatise*, which 'fell dead-born from the Press' (in his words), and the *Enquiry concerning Human Understanding*, which made him famous, may seem substantial to a close student now: but they are differences of emphasis, and in the persuasive manner of presentation, of the same few central ideas. Hume at least did not think of himself as finding his way, in his successive works, towards the solution of abstruse, or technical, problems. He wrote for an audience of intelligent amateurs, for the republic of letters. He aimed at elegance of arrangement, ease of manner, and at the virtues of the essayist, who treats of matters that should be of concern to all reflective men. The nature of knowledge and belief, and of moral distinctions, were not, as he viewed them, esoteric matters, even less were they academic. The natural setting of philosophical argument on these very abstract issues, as Hume conceived it, is not in a specialised department in a university: the setting is rather in the general flow of popular publications and current controversy. The problems neither ask for, nor admit, carefully refined solutions.

Why then is Hume, of all philosophers who have written in English, the most admired in British universities at the present time? This phenomenon requires explanation. When I began the study of philosophy in 1933, Hume's arguments were not taken seriously by most academic philosophers, particularly not in Oxford: they were dismissed as plausible sophistries, which the student was expected quickly to expose; and his conclusions were the mere extravagances of scepticism, with implications which no one could seriously accept. T. H. Green's Introduction to the *Treatise* had for several generations counted as a final demolition of this scepticism. Suddenly, in the late 1930s, all this, at least in England, changed.

The explanation, or part of it, is to be found in a new scepticism in recent philosophy, which is in some respects close to Hume's. In all his writings Hume tried to convince his readers that there can be no knowledge that can be called distinctively philosophical knowledge, no hope of rational insight into the structure of reality. A philosopher may study the anthropology of knowledge; he may describe the deep-rooted habits and customs which form our view of the external world and the system of our ordinary beliefs. For the rest, he can only remove the illusions and pretences of traditional philosophy: above all, the illusion that there must be some ultimate justification of our habits of thought, which is external to these habits themselves. There can be no Archimedean point outside our established habits of thought; our thinking is contained within them, because it is constituted by them; there is no possibility of stepping outside them and of judging them from some superior vantage-point. But exactly this had been the ancient ambition of philosophers: to find a criterion by which we can rectify our ordinary claims to knowledge, distinguishing the valid from the invalid claims before this superior tribunal.

That there can be no such superior tribunal has

also been one theme of contemporary analytical philosophy in Britain, beginning in the late 1930s and gaining strength since the war. Philosophy as a kind of anthropology of knowledge and belief is a conception revived in the later works of Wittgenstein. His suggestion was that we should turn attention to the justifications of belief, and of claims to knowledge, which are customarily accepted, and not look for a rationally satisfying justification altogether outside our established habits of thought : such a justification could never in principle be found. The proper work of philosophy is purely descriptive, to set out the linguistic facts that reveal our habits of thought, the facts that are always overlooked when too general, rational theories of knowledge are constructed. We must try also to uncover the motives that prompt philosophical theories, treating these theories as fantasies of reason, which can be understood and, by being understood, undermined. Hume also looked for the sources of metaphysical enthusiasm, for the type of mistake that we are making when we are inclined to claim some ultimate insight into the nature of things, an insight that is independent of experience.

Certainly there are important differences between this contemporary scepticism about the limits of philosophy and Hume's scepticism. Analytical philosophers today look for exactly stated distinctions between one kind of claim to knowledge and another. They find the sources of metaphysical pretences in the failure to notice a great variety of 'grammatical distinctions'. Hume dismissed any fine investigation of the meanings of words as of no philosophical importance. He considered only the general laws that govern the human imagination, and the formation of beliefs and sentiments, to be of proper concern to the philosopher. Philosophy for him was moral science, and he aspired to be the Newton of the moral sciences. The imagination has its laws, in accordance with which the impressions and ideas, the ultimate elements of experience, are invariably connected. Nature operates in a uniform manner to bind the fragments of experience together, as it is said to bind the particles of the physical universe into an intelligible system.

There is an intelligible system of the mind also, a cosmos of sentiment and belief; the several moral sciences will show the same laws of synthesis in the imagination everywhere at work : in our conception of persisting physical objects, of cause and effect, of virtue and vice, of justice and the rights of property. The general theory of the mind, expounded in the *Treatise* and, more simply, in the *Enquiry*, is a key that will open the lock of every one of the moral sciences. It was the application of a true understanding of human nature, with a view to a sane management of human affairs, that finally interested Hume, rather than pure philosophy, so-called.

We cannot today think of philosophy as this general science of the mind ; nor can we assume, like Hume, that there can be no difference of method between the natural sciences and any of the moral sciences. We cannot, because Kant stands between us and Hume. For Hume the ultimate appeal in any argument, whether it is a moral or a philosophical argument, whether it is a matter of politics or of aesthetics or of economics, is always an appeal to nature, to the regular order of our experience, to the normal course of things, as we actually observe them. Even questions of what ought to exist, and of what ought to be done, are ultimately to be settled by appeal to natural facts: in this case to the sentiments of approbation and of disapproval, of pleasure and displeasure, that are in fact common to mankind. Hume does not draw any absolute distinction between the rules to which our mind conforms itself in thought and behaviour, recognising them as rules to which any thinking *must* conform, and mere habits and uniformities in our thought and behaviour.

This distinction between rules and mere habits was the basis of Kant's philosophy. This was his answer to Hume's devastating scepticism, which had left ethics, logic and philosophy itself without forms of argument peculiar to themselves, and distinct from that of the natural sciences. Against Hume Kant argued that the human mind is the source of rules, which it imposes, both in thought and in action, on the raw material of experience. The proper work of philosophy is to make explicit the inner connexions between these rules that govern all our thought and action. Philosophical enquiry is therefore wholly different, both in its methods and in its aims, from any of the sciences. It is concerned with the presuppositions of knowledge and of judgement. The truths at which it arrives are necessary truths and not matters of fact. These necessary truths define the form and structure of human thought, and are not to be confused with the observations of anthropologists or psychologists.

7

British analytical philosophers of the present time sway uncertainly between Kant and Hume in the descriptions that they give of their own enquiries into the forms of language. Sometimes they write in Kantian terms, as if they are looking for the universal and necessary rules of language, rules that are the conditions of any coherent discourse at all : sometimes they write as if they are only describing the institution of language, as we find it, without any further claim that it must have the form that it does. It has not been, and still is not, easy to decide which of these descriptions is appropriate, since the nature of necessary truth is still not understood. Hume was formidably, reassuringly consistent in his naturalism ; but this consistency was purchased at the price of largely ignoring the foundations of logic and the development of mathematical knowledge. In the early eighteenth century it was easy to leave the truths of logic and mathematics on one side, with no full investigation of their nature. Today it is impossible for any empiricist philosopher, who otherwise accepts Hume's naturalism, to be as perfunctory as he was here. As Professor and Mrs. Kneale have shown in their recent book, *The Development of Logic*, logic is almost unique amongst the sciences in the unevenness of its development : a few great periods of discovery are followed by centuries of stagnation. From the publication of Frege's *Begriffsschrift* in 1879 until the present day, philosophers have lived through a great period of discovery in logic and in the foundations of mathematics ; and they can no longer cling to the simplified accounts of logical truth, and of necessary truths generally, which are to be found in Hume and John Stuart Mill. They cannot therefore be confident that philosophy, in its contemporary form of logical analysis, is only a peculiarly general kind of anthropology, the study of habits of thought and argument, the study of language as one institution among others; for there is always the suspicion that, in some sense of 'could', *some* of the forms of language could not be other than they are, that there is a contrast between rules of thinking that are unconditionally necessary and those that are merely customary, and that might be other than they are. The mere suspicion that there is such a contrast raises a problem which cannot be solved by the methods of science, or by attending to the data of experience; for the nature of fact and of experience, as opposed to possibility and necessity, are here in question. Anyone therefore who recognises the problem will segregate philosophy from the moral sciences, as having at least one problem peculiar to itself.

What then remains as a still living element of Hume's philosophy? I think — others will disagree — that he was the greatest moralist among British philosophers, the most subtle and the most profound: that he defined one consistent, and within its own terms, irrefutable, attitude to politics, to the problems of society, to religion; an attitude which is supremely confident and clear, that of the perfect secular mind, which can accept, and submit itself to, the natural order, the facts of human nature, without anxiety, and therefore without a

9

demand for ultimate solutions, for a guarantee that justice is somehow built into the nature of things. This philosophical attitude, because it is consistent and sincere, has its fitting style : that of irony, the style that exhibits as persuasively as possible both the demand for a complete solution of the problems and the frustration of this demand, and then finally leaves the matter there, with no further conclusion, no happy ending. From this point of view the *Dialogues concerning Natural Religion* is the summit of his achievement, and, second to that, the passage on scepticism concerning the senses in the *Treatise*. Some of the essays, particularly that on the perfect commonwealth, show the same two-sidedness, the same balancing between two contrary demands of human nature. In every aspect of their lives men are governed by their passions, of which reason both is, and ought to be, the slave.

Like his intimate friend — and, later, enemy — Rousseau, Hume represented Nature as operating through the heart, which has its own reasons, not through the intellect. But, less romantically, he believed that the calm passions may sometimes prevail, and that a sensible, cool calculation of happiness within the social order is both possible and desirable. His philosophy, his theory of knowledge, his ethics, and his political theory, are designed to persuade men to understand their passions, and thereafter calmly and without enthusiasm to make arrangements that they should live together peacefully and agreeably, in a decent compromise with the conflicting demands of their nature.

2

HUME'S EMPIRICISM AND MODERN EMPIRICISM

IN the *Enquiry concerning Human Understanding* Hume said :

If we take in our hands any volume ; of divinity or school metaphysics for instance ; let us ask : *Does it contain any abstract reasoning concerning quantity or number ?* No. *Does it contain any experimental reasoning concerning matter of fact or existence ?* No. Commit it then to the flames, for it can contain nothing but sophistry and illusion.[1]

In *Language, Truth and Logic* Professor Ayer quoted this passage, and asked :

What is this but a rhetorical version of our own thesis that a sentence that does not express either a formally true proposition or an empirical hypothesis is devoid of significance ? [2]

Hume realised that his philosophy provided a criterion of significance. For in *An Abstract of a Treatise of Human Nature* he said about himself :

When he (our author) suspects that any philosophical term has no idea annexed to it (as is too common), he always asks *from what impression that idea is derived ?* And if no impression can be produced, he concludes that the term is altogether insignificant.[3]

---

[1] *Enquiry concerning Human Understanding*, § XII, pt. iii.
[2] A. J. Ayer, *Language, Truth and Logic*, 2nd ed., 1950, p. 54.
[3] *Hume: Theory of Knowledge*, edited by D. C. Yalden-Thomson, 1951, p. 251.

This principle is closely related to the principle that Russell formulated in *The Problems of Philosophy* :

Every proposition which we can understand must be composed wholly of constituents with which we are acquainted.[1]

Hume's system even contains a psychological version of logical atomism. For example, in the *Enquiry* he compares his kind of analysis to microscopy :

Complex ideas may, perhaps, be well known by definition, which is nothing but an enumeration of those parts or simple ideas that compose them. But when we have pushed up definitions to the most simple ideas, and find still some ambiguity and obscurity ; what resource are we then possessed of ? By what invention can we throw light on these ideas, and render them altogether precise and determinate to our intellectual view ? Produce the impressions or original sentiments from which the ideas are copied. These impressions are all strong and sensible. They admit not of ambiguity. They are not only placed in a full light themselves, but may throw light on their correspondent ideas, which lie in obscurity. And by this means, we may, perhaps, attain a new microscope or species of optics, by which, in the moral sciences, the most minute and most simple ideas may be so enlarged as to fall readily under our apprehension, and be equally known with the grossest and most sensible ideas that can be the object of our enquiry.[2]

[1] Bertrand Russell, *The Problems of Philosophy*, 16th imp., 1936, p. 91.
[2] *Enquiry concerning Human Understanding*, § VII, pt. i.

Russell was thinking of a similar analogy when he said :

The reason that I call my doctrine *logical* atomism is because the atoms that I wish to arrive at as the sort of last residue in analysis are logical atoms and not physical atoms. Some of them will be what I call 'particulars' — such things as little patches of colour or sounds, momentary things — and some of them will be predicates or relations and so on. The point is that the atom I wish to arrive at is the atom of logical analysis, not the atom of physical analysis . . . The process of sound philosophising, to my mind, consists mainly in passing from those obvious, vague, ambiguous things, that we feel quite sure of, to something precise, clear, definite, which by reflection and analysis we find is involved in the vague thing that we start from, and is, so to speak, the real truth of which that vague thing is a sort of shadow.[1]

These are striking similarities, and it would be easy to add to the list. But how deep really is the affinity between Hume's empiricism and modern logical empiricism? Perhaps the most obvious difference is that the analysis that Hume practised was psychological or phenomenological, rather than logical. Consequently when he applied his theory of meaning to some difficult problem, like the idea of causal necessity, he searched his mind for an impression or set of impressions from which the idea could be derived. For he held that, if it were a genuine idea, it would either be derived directly from a single impression, which it copied, or else it would be built up by definition out of other ideas, each of which would itself have been derived from an impression. The result of his search in this case was that the idea is derived not from any sensory impression, but from an interior impression of inevitability. When someone makes a causal inference, he cannot help making it, since he is drawn along by the association of ideas. That, according to Hume, is the origin of the idea of causal necessity.

Few modern empiricists have taken over Hume's positive solution of this problem, but many have taken over his more important negative contention, that there is no sensory impression of causal necessity. They have taken it over and transformed it into a logical thesis. According to them, the connexion between a cause and its effect is not a third thing that is observable in the particular situation, and therefore every singular causal statement must be logically connected with some general causal statement. This is clearly a logical version of Hume's thesis that an inference from cause to effect depends on the association of the two ideas, which is itself produced by the constant conjunction of the two impressions to which they correspond.

But how much difference does this transformation really make? Certainly, at first sight, it seems to make a great difference. For the way in which Hume conducts his search for an impression of causal necessity makes it appear to be only a contingent fact that no such impression is yielded by the senses : and he sometimes talks as if it were only a contingent fact that the only possible connexion between distinct impressions is constant conjunction. The modern version, on the other hand, makes it quite clear that it is logically impossible that any third thing that might be observed between the cause and its effect should be the desired causal connexion, since any such third thing would merely lead us to ask how the cause was connected with it, and how it was connected with the effect, so that the problem that originally remained unsolved at one point would now remain unsolved at two points. It also demonstrates that a logical connexion between two events, which, according to it, is the only form of connexion that is stronger than constant conjunction, is simply ruled out by the requirement that the two events must be distinct. However, Hume was aware that his negative thesis is more secure than he sometimes makes it appear. For he says that those who object that there must be something more to causal necessity do not really know what they want; and here he comes very close to arguing that no sensory impression could conceivably be the desired impression of causal necessity, and that no connexion stronger than constant conjunction could conceivably link two distinct impressions.

Perhaps it is not so very important that Hume examined the contents of the mind, whereas modern empiricists examine language. It may be a more important difference that Hume's psychological system contains an over-simplification which is avoided in their logical system. For he often treats a thought as if it were merely an idea : but, in fact, if the word 'idea' is used in his sense, a complete thought can never be reduced to a single idea, since it is necessarily composed of at least two ideas. Similarly, a sentence, which expresses a complete thought, cannot be reduced to a single element (a word is usually a single element : but there are various exceptions to this : *e.g.* 'Ambulo' is a complete Latin sentence). Modern empiricists, who start with sentences, are careful to observe the distinction between them and the elements out of which they are composed. Unlike Hume, they do not treat the composite product as if it were a single unit.

An example of Hume's over-simplification can be found in his account of memory. According to him, all that happens when a person remembers something is that a strong and vivacious idea (*i.e.* image) of it occurs in his mind. This simple account seems to fit a case in which an image just comes into my mind, for example an image of a house that I visited as an infant, and I myself am unaware that it is a memory, but others assure me that it is. But suppose that we take another, more frequent type of case, for example a house that is later in my life, and I try to remember what kind of tree it was that stood on the lawn in front of it. Perhaps my effort of recollection would be rewarded by an image of a tulip-tree. Then this image would not be an isolated picture, which just came into my mind, as Hume suggests. On the contrary, it would be deliberately summoned up by me as part of a complete thought, the thought that a tulip-tree stood in front of that house. If the remainder of the thought consisted of images (and Hume has no other material to offer), the whole thing would be a proposition expressed in images, just as a sentence is a proposition expressed in words. When he reduces it to a single image, he is unable to explain what makes it a memory about a particular place. If he tried to meet this objection by saying that everything could be got into one image of the front view of the house, he would still have to admit that this image was divided into parts which were taken in a specific order, the order in which the thought would be expressed in words.

The same over-simplification can be seen at work in his account of existence. 'To reflect on anything simple', he says, 'and to reflect on it as existent are nothing different from one another. The idea of existence, when conjoined with the idea of any object, makes no addition to it. Whatever we conceive we conceive to be existent.'[1] This, of course, does not mean that whatever we conceive we believe to exist, since believing, as he was well aware, is more than conceiving. His point is that, when I consider the possibility that there is a weather-vane on top of that house, I think of the weather-vane as existing, without yet believing that it does exist. It is easy to see why he takes this view. For the original impression, to which the idea of the weather-vane corresponds, was not accompanied by a separate impression of existence.

However, this is not enough to establish his point. For, though existence is not a separate impression — *i.e.* not a property that things in the world are seen to possess — it might still be a separate idea. Indeed, if it were not, it is hard to see how anyone could have a negative existential thought, for example, the thought that God does not exist

[1] *Treatise*, Bk. I, pt. 2, § vi.

(whether he believed it or not). But Hume does not think of this. He uses the example of God's existence in order to reduce all complete thoughts to single ideas.

It is a vulgar error [he says] to distinguish conception from judgement; to define conception as the simple survey of one or more ideas, and to define judgement as the separating or uniting of different ideas. This distinction and these definitions are faulty. For it is far from true that, in every judgement that we form, we unite two different ideas; since in the proposition *God is*, or indeed any other which regards existence, the idea of existence is no distinct idea which we unite with that of the object, and which is capable of forming a compound idea by the union.[1]

But the error is Hume's. The idea of existence must be a separate idea, since otherwise nobody could have a negative existential thought. Admittedly, it is a peculiar idea, because it adds nothing to anything in the world, and so is not a predicate (an ambiguous thesis), and, no doubt, this peculiarity was one of the things that led Hume to conclude that complete thoughts are single ideas. But we can avoid this conclusion if we treat existence as an idea of a higher order — viz. the idea of an idea's having a correspondent impression or impressions,[2] or the concept of a concept's having an instance or instances. This, in effect, is how Kant and Russell treat existence. If we follow them, there will be no reason to expect the idea of existence to be derived from an impression in a straightforward way, and

---

[1] *Treatise*, Bk. I, pt. 3, § vii, footnote.
[2] Hume says that we have ideas of ideas. *Ibid*. Bk. I, pt. 1, § i.

the absence of such an impression will be perfectly explained.

In any case, there seems to have been no good reason why Hume should have extended his over-simplified account of existential thoughts to other thoughts. For other ideas do not possess the peculiarity of the idea of existence. Why, then, did he not treat existential thoughts as exceptional, and admit that other thoughts cannot be reduced to single ideas? Perhaps the reason is that he believed that he could treat all thoughts as if they were existential in form. For example, he may have regarded the thought that the tree in front of that house might be a tulip-tree as a single complex idea or image of something whose existence in the real world is automatically conceived with it. But there are many objections to this, the most obvious one being that it does not bring out the specific thing that the person is thinking (and would say, if he put his thought into words).

How is Hume's maxim, that all ideas are derived from impressions, related to Russell's maxim, that every proposition that we can understand must be composed wholly of constituents with which we are acquainted? Russell's point is that every proposition contains some terms whose meaning depends on their denotation, and that anyone who understands it must be acquainted either with the denotations of those terms or with the denotations of other terms into which they can be analysed. If Hume had not reduced complete thoughts to single ideas, his maxim would have come close to being a psychological version of Russell's: viz. in a significant thought every idea must either be derived directly from a single impression, or else it must be built up by definition out of other ideas, each of which would itself have been derived from an impression. But Hume did reduce complete thoughts to single ideas, as has been shown. In any case, even if he had not done so, his maxim would not have been an exact psychological counterpart of Russell's. For Hume's ideas are not unspoken words that denote impressions, as Russell's spoken words do, but images that copy impressions (though the extent to which general ideas can do this is limited).

Hume's psychological system has another deficiency, which is connected with his over-simplified account of complete thoughts, and that is that it does not allow for singular references that are not explicitly descriptive. For example, a proper name or a demonstrative pronoun may occur as the subject of a singular sentence, and a corresponding psychological element ought to occur in the thought that the sentence expresses. But all Hume's singular ideas have descriptive content, naturally enough, since they are copied from sensory impressions. Consequently, a singular thought, for example the thought that Richmond is on the river, will achieve its reference by means of an idea of Richmond, *i.e.* by means of an image which functions as a kind of description of the place.[1] The result is a thought which is rather like a proposition in which, according to Russell's recommendation, a definite description has been substituted for a proper name; except that in Russell's analysis it is clear which is the subject

[1] Cf. what he says about the idea of Paris. *Treatise*, Bk. I, pt. 1, § i.

of the proposition and which is the predicate, whereas in Hume's over-simplified account of thoughts the specific order in which their parts are to be taken is not clear.

But what about demonstrative pronouns? There seems to be no trace of them in Hume's system. The explanation of their disappearance is that they usually occur in sentences about things that are being perceived at the moment, and in his system there is no room for thoughts about things that are being perceived at the moment. If there had been room for such thoughts, they would have achieved their singular references in the usual Humean way, by means of ideas with descriptive content, and so there would still have been no exact psychological counterpart of demonstrative pronouns, which lack descriptive content, or almost entirely lack it. But in fact there is no room at all for such thoughts, because, though ideas can function, albeit inadequately, as thoughts that are not about contemporaneous sensory impressions, they cannot function at all as thoughts that are about contemporaneous sensory impressions. For, according to Hume, an idea can refer to an impression only by copying it, and what, for him, would be the point of copying a sensory impression that was being received at that moment? So demonstrative pronouns vanish without trace. It is not just that their psychological counterparts are subjected to analysis, which is what happens with proper names, but rather, in their case there is just no room in the system for their psychological counterparts, so that there is nothing there to be analysed.

His exclusion of all singular references that are not explicitly descriptive produces an important difference between his version of atomism and Russell's version. Of course, his version is psychological, and Russell's is logical. But, in addition to that difference, it is important that Hume develops an atomic theory only about general ideas, whereas Russell extends the theory so that it covers not only general terms but also singular terms. The explanation of Hume's restriction of his theory is that his system contains no psychological counterpart of non-descriptive singular terms, or — to put the same thing from a logical point of view — that it is more like Quine's system than Russell's. Consequently, his atomic theory can only be applied to general ideas. It may sound paradoxical to say this, since all his ideas are particular in their existence, and achieve generality, if they do achieve it, only by being given a general signification. But, though paradoxical, it is true. For generality and singularity are not intrinsic properties of ideas, but depend on the way in which ideas function in thinking. Now the function of one of his singular ideas, for example, the idea of Richmond, is to refer to a particular. But it will always perform this function through its descriptive content, and, since it must always be possible to describe a particular in more than one way, it follows that all singular ideas must be complex, and so the only ideas that could possibly be simple are general ones.

A general idea is simple, according to Hume, if it can be acquired only from a corresponding impression, and complex if it can also be built up by definition out of other ideas (singular ideas, because they can always be built up in this way, are always complex). Russell's distinction between simple and complex general terms runs parallel to this : a general term is simple if its meaning cannot be learned without acquaintance with its denotation, and complex if it can be defined, because in that case there will be an alternative way of learning its meaning, viz. acquaintance with the denotations of the terms that occur in its definition. Russell's extension of this theory to singular terms produced his theory of logically proper names, a theory which is fraught with interesting difficulties, but which has no analogue in Hume's system.

Hume never looked closely enough into the internal structure of thoughts, and he believed that he could treat them as single ideas. But he examined the connexions between them with great care, and his account of causal inference is the most important thing in the first book of the *Treatise*. Professor Hampshire has pointed out in his introductory essay [1] that it is not matched by an equally thorough account of *a priori* inference, and that it relies too heavily on the fact that it is natural for human beings to form habits of thought, and that these are two striking differences between Hume's philosophy and modern analytic philosophy.

When Hume uses habit to explain inference, he is, of course, not writing about *a priori* inference, but only about causal inference.

To consider the matter aright [he says], reason is nothing but a wonderful and unintelligible instinct in

[1] p. 8.

our souls, which carries us along a certain train of ideas, and endows them with particular qualities, according to their particular situations and relations. This instinct, it is true, arises from past observation and experience; but can anyone give the ultimate reason why past experience and observation produces such an effect, any more than why nature alone should produce it? Nature may certainly produce whatever can arise from habit: nay, habit is nothing but one of the principles of nature, and derives all its force from that origin.[1]

This paradox is not meant to apply to *a priori* reasoning. It is true that he allows himself to say that 'the necessity which makes two times two equal to four, or three angles of a triangle equal to two right ones, lies only in the act of the understanding by which we consider and compare these ideas.'[2] But he also says that such connexions between ideas are invariable so long as the ideas themselves remain the same.[3] So, when someone makes an *a priori* inference, the psychological process can be justified by the internal structure of the ideas themselves. In fact, his perfunctory account of *a priori* inference is a psychological version of the theory of analytic propositions. The central contention of the first book of the *Treatise* is, as Professor Ayer says, that *a priori* propositions are empty, and that any significant proposition that is not empty must be based on experience.[4]

Hume's account of causal inference is a subtle paradox. He is not proposing the naïve thesis that the association between the idea of the cause and

---

[1] *Treatise*, Bk. I, pt. 3, § xvi.   [2] *Ibid.*, § xiv.   [3] *Ibid.*, § i.
[4] Cf. *Enquiry concerning Human Understanding*, § IV, pt. i.

the idea of the effect always works instantly and
blindly in the mind of the person making the inference. Perhaps this does happen in simple and
obvious cases, but even then people can recall and
review the evidence which supports their inferences,
the constant conjunctions of the correspondent impressions. But in complicated cases the evidence is
often conflicting, and, according to Hume, reflection
on it is essential. He even allows that, when people
pause to assess the evidence in such cases, they in-
voke rules, and he gives a list of rules by which to
judge of causes and effects.[1] So his paradox is not
a piece of naïveté: he is not simply failing to allow
for the fact that people often pause and reflect on the
evidence that supports their causal inferences, and
consciously follow rules when they assess its direction
and strength.

But, if he allows all this, is there any room left
for his paradox, that causal inference depends on
the association of ideas? There is, but only if he
uses association to explain other operations of the
mind, instead of denying their existence. This, in
fact, is what he does. His rules — or at least those
of them that do not simply follow from the definitions of cause and effect — are themselves based on
experience, but on experience of a wider and more
general kind. But in his system this means that they
too are based on constant conjunctions of impressions.
Consequently, he can appeal in the usual way to the
association of ideas in order to explain the fact that
people accept rules — or, at least, those rules that
are not guaranteed by definitions.

[1] *Treatise*, Bk. I, pt. 3, § xv.

So the subtle point of his paradox is that the operations of the mind that assist causal inference, however various they may be, all depend for their justification on the same kind of evidence, constant conjunctions of impressions. This point is, of course, the negative thesis that many modern empiricists have taken over from Hume. But it is highly debatable whether the right way to make this point is to try to use one operation of the mind, association, to explain the others, as he does in his paradox. For why should there not be several irreducibly different operations, all based on the same kind of evidence? And, if his explanation were worked out in full psychological detail, could it possibly retain any plausibility? These are some of the considerations that have led most modern empiricists to reject his positive solution of the problem of causal necessity.

But Hume does not attempt to give any detailed justification of his contention that even people who are following a rule are merely being drawn along from one idea to another associated idea. In fact, as he implacably extends the word 'association' to cover more and more operations of the mind, it becomes clear that he is simply applying it to all connexions between ideas that are not justified by the internal structure of the ideas themselves. Then, having collected all the problematical phenomena under one heading, he says that the tendency to associate ideas is just a feature of human nature that has to be accepted without explanation. Or he sometimes allows that it might be worth looking for a physiological explanation of it.[1] Either way,

---

[1] *Treatise*, Bk. I, pt. 2, § v.

it is a brute fact about human beings that they record constant conjunctions in their experience.

A rational man (in the loose sense of that phrase) is a man who makes sure that the operations of his mind that cannot be justified *a priori* will always match the constant conjunctions in his experience. For obviously an operation is not justified merely by being one of those that Hume grouped together under the heading 'association': it also needs to match a constant conjunction. But, since the operations to which he gave this title do not in themselves provide a justification of inferences, there is no obvious reason why he should not have extended it still further to cover operations that assist *a priori* inferences, which are justified in an entirely different way. For such an extension would not have produced a collision between two incompatible justifications. Why, then, did he not make it? Perhaps he would have done so if his account of *a priori* inference had been less perfunctory, and if he had included an examination of complicated cases where the mind gropes from stage to stage in an argument, instead of confining himself to simple cases where the inner connexion between two ideas is grasped immediately. Or it may be that even then he would not have extended the operation of association to *a priori* inferences. For possibly it would have seemed to him absurd to say that a person had learned to associate a series of ideas each of which had an *a priori* connexion with the next one. But, in fact, it would not be absurd. For *a priori* inferences can become habitual no less than causal inferences: and, given his paradoxical extension of association to cases where someone is following a rule, there is no reason left why it should not be said to be at work even in cases where an *a priori* inference is accompanied by insight.

However, it may be that there is another, more interesting explanation of his refusal to extend association to *a priori* inferences. For he certainly believed that the theory of the association of ideas not only belongs to the descriptive psychology of human beings, but also provides part of the justification of causal inference. Of course, it could not possibly provide the whole justification, since associations have to match constant conjunctions: but it might well provide part of it, because it might be impossible to find a justification that did not appeal either to it or to some other very general fact about human beings. Now the tendency to associate is a contingent fact: it might have been otherwise. But Hume may have thought that the 'act of understanding', which is needed in *a priori* inference, and which is elicited in most people by certain pairs of ideas, is something that could not conceivably have been lacking in all people. If he thought this, his refusal to extend association to *a priori* inferences would be explained. For it would be natural for him to refuse to apply the same name to something that human nature might conceivably have lacked and to something that it could not conceivably have lacked.

But is it really true that human nature could not conceivably have lacked the capacity for Hume's 'acts of understanding', or — a less radical question — is it really true that they could not have been elicited by entirely different pairs of ideas from those that do in fact elicit them? Anyone who took the extreme conventionalist view of logical necessity would answer these questions, or at least the second one, in the negative. It is interesting to observe that when Wittgenstein takes this line in *Remarks on the Foundations of Mathematics*, he suggests that it is just an ultimate fact about human beings that they find certain *a priori* inferences natural. Thus he extends Hume's appeal to human nature from causal necessity to *a priori* necessity. Whether this extension of the appeal is correct or not, one thing at least is certain: the substitution of rules for habits does not do anything towards justifying an inference, unless it can be shown that the rules that people actually do follow are their own justification; but if this could be shown, it could equally be shown that their natural habits are their own justification.

Few modern empiricists would allow Hume to effect his extension of the word 'association' by vaguely diluting its meaning until it covers the following of rules. For they would have a precise objection to this: namely, that he says that when someone is drawn along from one idea to another associated idea, this process is itself causal, whereas the following of a rule is not a causal process. This objection was frequently used by Hume's British Idealist critics. If its point were simply that there is a clear difference between drawing a conclusion after careful reflection and drawing a conclusion automatically without reflection, it would be valid, but not a very damaging criticism of Hume. If the point is to be really damaging, it must be that the following of a rule cannot be regarded as a causal process from any point of view, not even from the point of view of an observer, who might be a psychologist or a neuro-psychologist. But is this thesis valid? It is not possible to give a quick answer.

3

HUME'S THEORY OF THE PASSIONS

THERE is no question of importance, whose decision is not comprised in the science of man; and there is none which can be decided with any certainty, before we become acquainted with that science.

This statement, made by Hume in the Introduction to his *Treatise of Human Nature*, reveals quite clearly the general standpoint from which he approached the main questions of philosophy; and it is in the light of his adoption of this position that all that he says in his major philosophical works must finally be judged and understood. Certainly, Hume was at one with his predecessors in holding that philosophy in *some* sense represents the most fundamental form of human enquiry, logically if not historically prior to all other disciplines. But he differed from many of them in his view of the character and purpose of philosophical investigation, and therefore in his conception of the way in which it could legitimately be considered to occupy a privileged position. To reach a true understanding of human nature, of the mental attributes and powers that human beings universally share and manifest: this is the proper and indispensable task of philosophy in so far as it can be said to explore the foundations, not merely of mathematics and the physical sciences (both of which are 'in some measure dependent on the science of *man*'), but also of what Hume called the 'moral subjects' — that is, ethics, politics, aesthetics and the general 'art of reasoning' or logic.

Hence it is apparent from the outset that Hume — although he himself did not use the word — regarded the type of undertaking upon which he was engaged as 'psychological'. Since he wrote he has been criticised by philosophers of varying schools and persuasions for the 'psychologism' which infects his treatment of cardinal issues in logic and the theory of knowledge; yet, however misguided his method may now appear to have been, it is as well to remember that he employed it quite deliberately, in the full realisation of what he was doing and in the belief that his procedure was capable of throwing light on areas of thought previously shrouded in darkness or confusion. It was not merely that, of all the things we may desire to know, the contents and workings of our own minds are those most directly and immediately available for our inspection and about which we are consequently least liable to form erroneous opinions. It also seemed to him clear that, by making them the prime object of its investigations, philosophy would become a study securely grounded upon experience and observation : it could thus furnish agreed solutions to the problems with which it had to deal, and would no longer be the source of unverifiable hypotheses and irresolvable disputes of the sort that had hitherto given 'metaphysical reasonings' so bad a name. The 'science of man' in Hume's sense would, in fact, involve the application to the human mind of those 'experimental methods' which had already proved to be of such immense consequence in the interpretation of phenomena in the physical world : as he himself put it, it was impossible to form any notion of the powers and qualities of the mind 'otherwise than from careful and exact experiments, and the observation of those particular effects, which result from its different circumstances and situations'. By this means we can hope to arrive at certain 'universal principles' governing human nature, and with the discovery of such principles we may — and, indeed, must — rest content. For, Hume thought, we manifestly cannot 'go beyond experience', and the quest for any further, metaphysically ultimate, explanation of the phenomena under discussion, over and above that which experience is capable of providing, will inevitably be vain.

In the first book of his *Treatise*, called 'Of the Understanding', Hume was concerned (generally speaking) with trying to uncover the operations of the human mind as these relate to our most basic forms of reasoning and belief. In the course of it he asks, and tries to answer, such questions as how we come to have the assurance we do have in the existence of an objective reality external to ourselves, what it is that leads us to think of events as being causally connected with one another, and (again) what underlies our conception of ourselves as identical continuing individuals, separate from the flux of ever-changing experiences which form the sole ingredients of consciousness. This does not, however, by any means exhaust the scope of his enquiry, and in the second book he turns to a different aspect

of his subject. Even when he is specifically considering the nature of our knowledge of the world, Hume
makes it clear that he thinks that reason, properly
understood, plays a much smaller rôle in our thought
than previous philosophers have supposed it to play,
and throughout his discussion he is anxious to stress
the importance of the imagination and of non-
rational propensities in determining the ways in
which we comprehend our experience. And there
is, in any case, a further point of great significance.
For we are not detached or purely contemplative
beings, confined in our interests to indulging a
capacity for theoretical cognition and ratiocination.
It is also obvious that we respond practically to
the things and persons that surround us and to the
circumstances in which we find ourselves placed :
we have, for instance, wants and desires which we
endeavour to satisfy by acting upon or altering our
environment ; moreover, in our dealings with our
fellows we recognise, and (sometimes, at least) are
guided by, feelings and considerations of the type
described as 'moral'. Here then, Hume was aware,
there lay a whole area of human nature which had
to be explored if his account was to be at all adequate ; and, as a first requirement, it was necessary
to examine, carefully and in detail, what he referred
to as 'the passions, and other emotions resembling
them'.

Despite the differences in the topics involved,
Hume was none the less insistent that his treatment
of 'the subjects of the understanding and passions'
formed 'a complete chain of reasoning by themselves'.
And certainly there were evident similarities in

the approach and method he employed in the two cases. For example, in Book I of the *Treatise* Hume divides the basic constituents of human consciousness into two main classes; into, first, 'impressions', and, secondly, 'the faint images of these in thinking and reasoning' which he termed 'ideas'. When he comes to discuss the passions in Book II the terminology of 'impressions and ideas' is once again prominent. The class of impressions is now, however, subdivided into two further categories — there are 'external' and 'internal' impressions. By 'external', Hume chiefly means impressions which come to us through the senses (though he also includes 'bodily pleasures and pains'); by 'internal', he means phenomena associated with introspection (or 're-flection') rather than perception — what, in other words, might loosely be called 'states of mind': thus a feeling of heat or cold is an 'external' impression, while to experience grief or fear is to be aware of an 'internal' one. In one sense, however, impressions of both kinds stand 'originally on the same footing': all are conceived (initially, at any rate) 'atomistically', as separate, discrete, independent existences, rather as if they could be regarded as the mental equivalents of the material particles of physical theory. But, while impressions (and also ideas) are 'distinct', it does not follow that they exhibit no kind of coherence or order; and this brings us to another central tenet of Hume's general conception of the mind and its workings, one that plays an especially important part in his theory of the passions.

'It is sufficient for my purpose', he wrote in his

later *Dissertation on the Passions*, 'if I have made it
appear that, in the production and the conduct of
the passions, there is a certain regular mechanism,
which is susceptible of as accurate a disquisition, as
the laws of motion, optics, hydrostatics, or any part
of natural philosophy'. The 'regular mechanism'
referred to is the famous principle of the *association
of ideas*, the operations of which Hume elsewhere
explicitly compared to those of the Newtonian principle of gravitation in the natural realm : thus he
spoke in the *Treatise* of 'a kind of *Attraction*, which
in the mental world will be found to have as extraordinary effects as in the natural, and to show itself
in as many and as various forms'. In the light of
much that he says we should, in fact, expect Hume
to present the inner world of our passions and emotions on analogy with a closed physical or mechanical
system, wherein phenomena are produced and dis-
place one another according to certain invariant
'associative' laws that operate (so he asserts) by
means of 'resemblance, contiguity and causation'.
And, to a considerable extent, this expectation is
fulfilled. Thus, as an example of the way in which
the relation of resemblance links particular emotions
together, he claims that grief and disappointment
give rise to anger, anger gives rise to envy, envy to
malice, and malice to grief again — 'till the whole
circle be completed'. He also attempts to demonstrate, in the course of an extremely lengthy and
intricate discussion, how the various associative
mechanisms combine to produce and direct a
group of very common passions ; namely, pride,
humility, love and hate. As a useful illustration of

Hume's typical method of analysis, it is worth considering, very briefly, what he says about the first of these.

Pride, Hume states, is in itself a 'simple and uniform impression'; like the rest of the passions, we cannot give a 'just definition' of it verbally, but simply recognise it as a specific feeling. We can, however, specify 'such circumstances as attend' its occurrence. In the first place it is clear (Hume thinks) that the *object* of pride is always ourselves: as he rather quaintly puts it, 'according as our idea of ourselves is more or less advantageous, . . . we are elated by pride, dejected by humility'. Secondly, the general *causes* of pride can be identified. What makes us feel proud is always some person or thing intimately related to ourselves, and it does so in virtue of one or more characteristics which it possesses and which give us pleasure. If, to take an instance, one is proud because one owns a beautiful house, the object of one's pride is oneself, while what makes one feel proud is both the fact that the house is one's own and the fact that it is beautiful and therefore a source of personal pleasure. Hume now undertakes to show why all this should be so. So far as the object of pride is concerned, he suggests that it is simply a matter of empirical or natural fact, universally established, that the passion of pride 'fixes on', or 'produces', the 'idea of self'. In the case of its causes things are more complicated. For here there is a double association between impressions and ideas at work: on the one hand, an association between the pleasure we take in (say) the beauty of our house and the agreeable sensation of pride itself; on the other, an association between the idea of what belongs to us (the house) and the idea of ourself (as the 'natural' object of all pride). In this way we can see how it is that 'anything that gives a pleasant sensation, and is related to self, excites the passion of pride', the key to the solution lying in the twin operation of laws of association which are here said mutually to reinforce one another.

Hume did not — as certain later Utilitarians (notably James Mill) may be said to have done — seek to explain or derive all passions and emotions through association. He distinguished, for example, between 'direct' and 'indirect' passions. Hunger, lust, benevolence towards friends and resentment towards enemies were of the former type, and they were considered by him to arise from 'a natural impulse or instinct which is perfectly unaccountable'. But even when regarded as applying only to the limited class of 'indirect' passions, Hume's procedure seems somewhat curious. In his account of pride, for instance, he writes most of the time as if pride were an agreeable feeling in the mind which can be picked out and named independently of its objects or alleged general 'causes'; he speaks, too, as if it were experience and observation alone which make apparent its connexion with things that please us or stand in some close relation to us. On Hume's view of the matter it would appear to be at least *intelligible* to talk of a man feeling proud of something which bore no special relation to himself or towards which he entertained feelings of utter repugnance; it is just the case that, human nature being what it is and the psychological laws of association being what they are, such an eventuality could never occur. But it may reasonably be asked whether this is really so, and whether the 'circumstances' which Hume treats as being only empirically related to the phenomenon of pride as its exciting causes do not, on the contrary, constitute part of its very essence. For if the conditions Hume mentions were not satisfied, could we intelligibly speak of pride at all?

This is not a trivial objection, to be passed over or lightly brushed aside. Rather, it underlines part of a more general difficulty that is raised by Hume's entire treatment of the passions as the isolable contents of a direct introspective awareness. Even if we disregard those more subtle attitudes of mind or states of feeling which appear to elude neat labels or tidy classification, it seems clear that our ordinary loves and hates, hopes and fears, fits of anger or remorse, cannot plausibly be interpreted as mere impressions or 'inward' sensations, describable without reference to the objects towards which they are directed and in distinction from any of the forms of outward expression in which they typically manifest themselves. Hume himself showed at times a partial recognition of this point : he noticed, for example, that 'love and hate are not completed within themselves . . . but carry the mind to something farther' — love is characterised by a desire for the happiness of the person loved, hate by an opposite tendency. And he considered the 'hypothesis' that such desires are necessarily comprised within the ideas of love and hatred, are

39

included in their very meaning; only, however, to reject it in favour of the alternative view, more consonant with his general position, that here, once again, we have a purely contingent connexion — the desires in question are 'only conjoined with' love and hatred by 'the original constitution of the mind'. It is, he writes, perfectly conceivable that the connexion might be reversed: 'I see no contradiction in supposing a desire of producing misery annexed to love, and of happiness to hatred', its being merely an empirical fact that this is not so.

Such examples make clear the tenacity with which Hume was prepared to stick to his original programme. In his attempt to treat the passions as discrete experiences he exhibits a persistent tendency to construe the implications of what are in fact logically complex notions in terms of correlations between atomistically conceived impressions: these correlations might imaginably be other than they are, and it is through experience alone that we learn of their existence. Hence the strangely truistic character of many of his conclusions regarding the springs of human feeling and motivation, the obstinately *a priori* air that clings to propositions put forward as though they represented scientific discoveries about human nature, while in reality being nothing of the kind. In the light of what we had been led to expect from Hume's talk of the application of 'careful and exact experiments' to the study of the mind, it is all a little disappointing.

To a large extent Hume was the victim of a philosophical inheritance that partly derives from Descartes. As the foremost representative of 'British empiricism' it may at first sight appear odd to suggest that he owed anything to a Continental philosopher whose name is perhaps most generally associated with a profoundly sceptical attitude towards sense-experience and to claims to knowledge founded upon it. Further, were not some of Hume's most devastating arguments directed against the Cartesian conception of the mind or 'soul' as a non-bodily substance, with an existence independent of its particular states and acts? Yet in his theory of the passions Hume retained many of the assumptions that underlie Descartes' own book on the subject, *Les Passions de l'âme*. For Descartes, too, such things as fear, sadness, pity and anger were 'things we experience in ourselves' — immediate objects of introspection that refer to nothing beyond themselves and about which we cannot be mistaken in our judgements. And Hume in effect follows Descartes in sharply dividing the mind from the body; the relation between inwardly felt passions and emotions and their manifestations in overt behaviour is a purely contingent one, discovered by experience. It was on the basis of such contentions, supplemented by a sensationalist vocabulary and an associationist methodology, that Hume tried to construct a psychological science in parallel with Newtonian physics. Admittedly, his practice was not always consistent with his theory. Thus at crucial points, particularly when discussing what he called the 'calm' as opposed to the 'violent' passions, references to 'settled principles of action' and to 'predominant inclinations in the soul' find their way into his account: notions that are not easily accommodated within a picture which presents our mental life as being essentially a sequence of passive impressions and ideas following one another or combining in recurrent patterns. Yet Hume never openly disavowed the theory, and his fidelity to its fundamental presuppositions was matched by that of a long line of other philosophers and psychologists stretching from his own time onwards. It is true that sporadic attacks upon these presuppositions were made in the nineteenth century by thinkers who lay outside the main empiricist tradition; for example, by Maine de Biran, Schopenhauer and Nietzsche. Nevertheless, it is only comparatively recently that they have come to be systematically challenged; not merely from the side of philosophical analysis and criticism, but also from the direction of observational enquiry and research — developments both in behaviourist approaches to psychology and in Freudian psycho-analysis have (in very different ways) underlined their inadequacy. Whatever its other shortcomings, the conception of a 'science of man' on the lines envisaged by Hume and his successors had a remarkably long career.

4

HUME ON PERSONAL IDENTITY

A PERSON is sometimes said to have no strong sense of his own identity. What that usually means is that he lacks some of the things that give inner stability and continuity to a human life : for instance, he may be uncertain about his beliefs, feelings and desires ; he may not know the sort of person that he is, or the sort of person that he wants to be. But there is also another way in which a person may lose the sense of his own identity : he may be afflicted with amnesia and simply forget who he is. Someone in this situation would probably need the help of the police in order to re-establish his own identity, and, of course, he would want them to tell him not only the sort of person that he was, but also the particular person that he was. These two pieces of information are connected with one another, and in Nigel Dennis's novel *Cards of Identity* the victims are deprived of both at once. But it is easy to see that they are different things, and the philosophical problem of personal identity is in fact concerned with only one of them — particular identity.

Most people know their own particular identities. I know who I am, and I can produce enough facts to establish who I am. Anyone who wonders what these facts would be in his own case has only to imagine himself being questioned by the police.

But what about other people? Every day I see a great number of other people whose particular identities are unknown to me. So there is a striking contrast between one's knowledge of one's own particular identity and one's knowledge of the particular identities of other people. But it is not such a complete contrast as it seems to be at first sight. For though I know enough facts to establish my own particular identity, there are also a great many facts of this kind that I do not know. For example, I know my name, address and telephone number, but I do not know whether I am the person who walked through the gate of this college exactly twenty-nine minutes ago.

The philosophical problem of personal identity is concerned with particular identities. It begins when one asks how such statements of personal identity are established. But that is only the beginning. For suppose that some philosopher gave a completely satisfactory account of the criteria that we use in order to establish that these statements are true. Then it would still be possible for someone to argue, in a sceptical way, that those criteria were inadequate, because they did not really add up to anything that could properly be called identity. This is how Hume's treatment of the problem develops. And other developments are possible: for instance, it might be argued that the real person is the soul, and that the real criteria of personal identity have nothing to do with the body. But whatever happens in the end, we can at least insist that any philosophical treatment of this subject should begin with a realistic account of the ways in which we ask and answer questions about the particular identities of people. After all, that is what it is all about.

Hume's treatment of the subject is surprisingly unrealistic. His account of the way in which questions of personal identity are asked and answered is out of touch with the familiar facts which ought to have been its starting-point. In everyday life one asks questions not only about one's own identity but also about the identities of other people. But Hume only considers questions about his own identity. It is true that he intends that what he says about himself should be applied by his readers to themselves. But this does not alter the situation. For each of his readers will consider the problem only in its application to his own case, as Hume himself does. So though Hume's use of the pronoun 'I' is, in a way, impersonal, it always excludes consideration of other people. That is very unrealistic. So too is his account of the way in which questions of personal identity are answered. For he never mentions the fact that we use physical criteria in answering them, but always confines himself to facts about the inner life of the person concerned. We might take the example that I gave just now and use it again in order to show how crippling these two limitations are. Suppose that I wish to establish that I am not the person who walked through the gate of this college exactly twenty-nine minutes ago. Then Hume would perhaps allow that I might do it by recalling what time it was when I entered this college. But this is not the only way of establishing that I am not that person. For I might get someone else to testify that my body has been in this room for more than twenty-nine minutes, and thus establish an alibi. And this alibi would bring in both the things that are missing in Hume's account — the use of physical criteria in answering identity-questions, and the posing of identity-questions about other people (since my witness poses an identity-question about me).

When Hume looked in his own mind for the criteria of his identity as a person, he found only a succession of impressions and ideas, related to one another in various ways. He failed to find any impression of the self that is supposed to have these impressions and ideas. He took this failure to be of the utmost importance. For he assumed that, if his adversaries were correct in thinking that the self is a mental substance, perhaps a soul, in which impressions and ideas inhered, then there would have to be a separate impression of the self. But there is no such impression, and therefore the continued identity of a person could only consist in certain relations between the impressions and ideas that were the contents of his mind.

These relations between impressions and ideas were, according to him, similarity and causation. It sounds very odd to our ears when we hear Hume saying that the continued identity of a person consists in the fact that his impressions and ideas form a series in which many of the elements are related by similarity and causation. But we have to remember that he is speaking from the eighteenth century in antique psychological terms. If we express his thesis in a different terminology, it sounds less odd. For it is quite natural to say that the continued identity of a person consists in the fact that his mental life contains many repetitions, and that its development is governed by causal laws.

How would these facts be used by someone who was trying to answer a question about the particular identity of a person? Perhaps it is not immediately clear how he would use them. If he were asking the other question that I mentioned at the beginning of this essay, the question whether a person's life had inner stability and continuity, it is very obvious how he would use them. For stability and continuity depend, to a large extent, on recurrent patterns and consistent developments of thought and feeling. But suppose that I were wondering about a question of particular identity; for example, whether a man talking to me on a railway journey was the man who talked to me several weeks ago in the station buffet. How would I use Hume's two factors? I think that they would make some contribution towards the solution of my problem. For example, the man might say things that fitted the character revealed in the earlier conversation. If he did, that would not *prove* that he was the same man, since two different people can have similar characters and views. In fact, the possibility of very extensive similarities, both psychological and psychical, between two different people creates a difficulty which can be completely overcome only by appealing to space, time and motion, as is done by people who produce alibis. Nevertheless consistency of character is some help in answering questions of particular identity.

Hume was dissatisfied with his two factors, but the reason for his dissatisfaction was not the difficulty that is presented by the possibility of extensive similarities, and so he was not led to recognise the importance of space, time, and motion which are, of course, involved in the physical criteria of personal identity. His reason for feeling dissatisfied was not that a statement of particular identity might turn out to be false in spite of the fact that his two criteria had been fulfilled — for example, that the travelling companion might not be the same man again after all — but rather that, whoever the man was, there would be something inadequate about his psychological history. For he thought that, though what he had said about the psychological history of a person was the very most that a careful empiricist could say, nevertheless it was inadequate, since it did not add up to anything that could properly be called identity. All that he had found was a series of impressions and ideas. Although the series itself lasted as long as the life of the person, it contained no permanent element; indeed, all its elements were so brief as to be almost momentary. It is true that the series as a whole exhibited various kinds of pattern and structure, but it had no background and no observer, rather like a piece of music in empty space. And Hume did not think that this was enough to deserve the name 'personal identity.' It might, indeed, be *called* personal identity, but only by courtesy and as a kind of fiction.

Now it might be thought that Hume was not entirely sincere when he expressed himself dissatisfied with his own theory of personal identity. For it is characteristic of his philosophy to take a generally accepted idea and to demonstrate that its foundation in human experience is inadequate. Of course, if it had no foundation at all, he would reject it completely. But what usually happens is that he finds adequate support only for a very reduced version of the original idea. And when he expresses dismay at the difference between the reduced idea, which is well founded, and the original idea, which is ill founded, he is usually being ironical, and he is implying that the original idea is largely pretentious nonsense. This kind of irony is very noticeable in his account of perception, and in his treatment of causal necessity. And it might be thought that there is a good deal of the same irony in his expression of dissatisfaction with his theory of personal identity, particularly since the theory was in conflict with an accepted religious doctrine. But this would be a complete misinterpretation. In the appendix to the *Treatise* he makes it absolutely clear that he regards his account of personal identity as totally unsatisfactory; and yet he confesses that he has nothing better to put in its place.

His total withdrawal of his theory of personal identity is neglected by some commentators, who talk as if he had made up his mind on the subject once and for all. But the withdrawal is a fact, and an important one. For if we look at his philosophy as a whole, we see that it has a serious consequence. His philosophy is, for the most part, neither abstract nor remote from human interests. It ranges very widely over morality, politics, aesthetics and religion.

In all this he constantly appeals to the idea of the self. But the idea of the self was precisely the idea that he was unable to place on an adequate foundation. So there is an important weakness, a weakness which he himself admits, in the theoretical basis of his science of human nature.

What exactly was the weakness? Hume gave his account of it in the appendix to the *Treatise*. But it is arguable that his diagnosis was wrong, and that the weakness was really something other than what he took it to be. So in the remainder of this essay I shall be occupied with two things. First, I shall try to explain Hume's version of what was wrong with his theory of personal identity : and then I shall argue that what is really wrong with it is something else, which he himself did not recognise.

First let us look at his own diagnosis of his failure. Now it is an important fact about him that he wished to achieve in the science of human nature what Newton had achieved in astronomy. Where Newton used mechanics, he would use what we now call psychology, and he compares his law of the association of ideas with Newton's law of gravitation. I think that the fact that he regarded his work in this way really explains why he was willing to reduce the accepted idea of causal necessity and the accepted idea of a material object, and yet could not bring himself to reduce the accepted idea of personal identity. For he was prepared, or at least half prepared, to reduce the external world to phenomena in the human mind. But this meant that his theory of the self had to bear a great weight, and so it was essential that it should remain strong and unreduced.

But when he reviewed it in the appendix to the *Treatise*, it seemed to him to be too thin and weak. He said that, if the self were a substance in which impressions and ideas inhered, or if there were a real connexion between impressions and ideas, he would be satisfied. But since neither of these two things was the case, he remained dissatisfied.

But would he really have been in a better position if he had been able to say that the self is a substance, or that there is a real connexion between impressions and ideas? Certainly he might have claimed to have justified the sense that we have of the stability and continuity of our lives. On the other hand, perhaps he would not have felt the need for some unattainable kind of connexion between the elements in our psychological histories if he had realised the importance of intentional connexions, instead of being so preoccupied with mechanical ones. However, suppose that he had succeeded in establishing one of the two things which, according to him, could not be established. Would that have helped him to solve the philosophical problem of the particular identity of persons? As I pointed out earlier, some of the factors that give stability and continuity to a human life can be used by a person who asks himself a question of particular identity. So this might be true of the two factors that Hume wished that he could find, but admitted that he could not find. Whether it would in fact be true is a difficult question, which I shall not attempt to answer here.

In any case, there is another deficiency in Hume's theory. He not only does not find adequate criteria for answering questions of particular identity, but also fails to provide a setting in which such questions can even be asked. This came about in the following way. When he asked himself a question about his own particular identity, he always confined himself to earlier impressions and ideas, and did not consider earlier speech, behaviour and actions. Perhaps he could have avoided this restriction, but it was at least very natural for a philosopher who admitted that he could give no rational account of our belief in the physical world. Anyway, the consequence was that he would ask himself whether, for example, he was the person who had a certain idea, which was not expressed in words, on New Year's Day 1735. But the trouble with this kind of question was that, if he had any reason to believe that the idea occurred at all, he could not fail to believe that it occurred in the series that was himself, David Hume. For only his own unaided memory vouched for the occurrence of the idea. Consequently he could never be in a position in which he could ask himself whether he was the person who . . .: if he had any doubt about the answer, he would equally doubt whether the question was properly framed.

This situation can be avoided only if questions of particular identity are framed in such a way that they make some reference to speech, behaviour and actions, or, more generally, to the body and its history. It is exceedingly important that this is so even when the identity-question is one that a person asks about himself. For example, when I ask myself whether I am the person who walked through the gate of this college at a particular moment today, I must have some way of knowing that there was such a person even if he was not myself. And that means that I must be able to use something other than my memory of my own psychological history. Otherwise there will be no possibility of my knowing that there was such a person unless he was myself. Questions of particular personal identity presuppose the existence of other people. If other people did not exist, there would be nobody for me not to be. And I must have some way of knowing that other people exist.

Now we are aware of other people only through their bodies. Whether this is a contingent fact or a necessary fact, it is the human predicament. And since we are in this predicament, any philosophical theory of personal identity must be based on our physical existence in space and time. That is absolutely essential. But what Hume tried to do was to work out a theory of personal identity that did not rely on our knowledge of the external world or on our awareness of other people. In this he necessarily failed, not only because he could not explain completely how questions of personal identity are answered, but because he could not explain at all how they are asked.

Hume was not a solipsist, but he suffered from a tendency to solipsism. As always happens in such a case, the attempt to describe the internal world without the external world led to a curious distortion. For Hume's impressions and ideas gradually began to take over the characteristics of material objects. In his discussion of personal identity he talked as if they could exist in isolation, floating in a kind of impersonal medium. And his version of the theory that the self is a substance, which he is reluctantly forced to reject, is based on obvious analogies with the body. When the external world is neglected, it usually makes itself felt in this way.

Earlier in this essay I said that Hume's theory of personal identity is unrealistic. That is true. It is unrealistic because it fails to take account of the fact that we live together in space and time, and communicate through our bodies. But though this is a true judgement about Hume's theory, it is an inadequate one. For it is not as if he simply overlooked these obvious facts through carelessness. If that were so, his theory would be of little interest. What makes it interesting is that it is a careful attempt to work out a theory of personal identity within an egocentric framework. The attempt failed, conspicuously and avowedly, because Hume was more consistent and clear-sighted than others who tried to do the same thing. That kind of failure is important. What it probably shows is that the thing cannot be done.

5

HUME ON CAUSATION

Hume's examination of the ideas of cause and
effect in his *Treatise of Human Nature* is
lengthy and elaborate, and justly celebrated.
It is, of course, very far from complete; and one
may wish that Hume had shown more awareness
than he does of the fact that this is so. He does not
explicitly distinguish, for instance, between *general*
causal statements — such as that heating causes
metals to expand — and *singular* ones — such as
that, on a particular occasion, the sun's heat caused
distortion in a section of railway track. Equally he
appears to take no account of the variety of items
which may be cited as causes and effects — for
instance, actions, happenings, changes, processes,
permanent states, objects, failures to act, or non-
occurrences. Hume announces his topic, baldly and
uninformatively, as 'the relation of cause and effect';
and when he has occasion to refer to those things
which are, or may be said to be, causes and effects,
he calls them, vaguely and undiscriminatingly,
'objects'.

But, although a certain pervasive neglect of quite
substantial distinctions leads Hume to say a number
of things about causes and effects which, taken in the
general, unqualified terms in which he states them,
cannot possibly be true, this perhaps does not matter
very much. It does not affect, I think, his central

contention. And it is this central contention that I want to consider in this essay — because, although nowadays it seems to be very widely accepted, I am inclined to think it is accepted rather too easily. What Hume is saying is a good deal more odd than is often realised.

Hume was writing on this subject in the 1730s; and though he had in mind a number of distinguished philosophers from whose accounts of causation he strongly dissented, I think his views can most illuminatingly be set in contrast with those of Locke, as published in his *Essay* in 1690.

Locke thought that, although there were certainly plenty of cases in which we could establish that two phenomena, A and B, were causally connected, there were few cases if any in which we could *understand the connexion* — in which, that is, we could see why A was the cause of B, or why, if A should occur, B *must* ensue. He thought this was so for two quite different reasons, which I shall illustrate with examples.

First, take the proposition that heating lead to about 600° Fahrenheit causes it to melt. Locke thought that we could find this to be so, but could not understand *why*. Well, why can't we understand? In Locke's view, the difficulty here is really a practical one. The observable properties of lead, he says, including its liability to melt if heated to the right degree, really depend on its atomic parts — there is, he assumes, a fundamental mechanical structure in the substance called 'lead' which determines its reaction to all contingencies, as, for instance, to heating; but, he then pessimistically

reflects, this fundamental structure is so very minute
that we have no prospect of ever discovering just
what it is. In the case of a clock, we can discover
by watching it that, when the minute hand points
to twelve, it strikes the hour : we can also, by careful
inspection of the works inside, see *why* this happens,
why it has to strike the hour when the hand is in
that position. But in the case of lead, this second
road is closed to us ; its inner works are far too
small to be inspected, and so we can never see *why*,
if heated to 600°, it then has to melt.

Second, a quite different case. We know, Locke
says, that an appropriate physical stimulus trans-
mitted via the sense-organs and nervous system to
the brain causes the person whose brain it is to have
a certain sensation — for instance, to see a blue
flash. But we cannot understand *why* this should be
so. Well, once again, why not ? Not, in this case,
because the explanatory mechanism is too minute
for us to inspect its workings, but simply because
there is no explanatory mechanism : it just *is the
case*, as a matter of bare, brute fact, that certain
sensations are the effects of certain physical stimuli ;
we cannot tell how or why they should be, because
there is just no intelligible, non-arbitrary connexion
between such diverse items as physical stimuli and
sensations. When my brain is stimulated *thus*, I see
a blue flash ; but if we ask why, we can answer only
that it has pleased God so to arrange matters.

Thus, in Locke's view, there are these two distinct
types of discoverable causal connexion, though
neither is *understandable* : in the one case there
simply is no intelligible link between the cause and

the effect: in the other case, although we can be sure that there is an, in principle, intelligible link, it is in fact inaccessible to us because the mechanism involved is too minute for observation.

Now it is, I believe, Hume's central contention that Locke was quite wrong in supposing these cases to be different. In his view, all cases of causal connexion are ultimately just like the connexion between a brain stimulus and the seeing of a blue flash: we can establish, if we are lucky, that the connexion holds; but we cannot say why it should hold, why the cause must produce that effect rather than some other. It is not that, as Locke thought, an explanatory link between the cause and its effect is sometimes missing, and sometimes in practice not discoverable; it is always missing; or rather, in no case is there any such thing. What we call a 'connexion' is really nothing more than a conjunction: causes and effects go together, but are in no other sense 'connected'.

It is important to be quite clear what is going on at this point. Hume is not denying, of course, that there is a sense in which it is true that lead's property of melting when heated 'depends on' its atomic structure; he would presumably have regarded this as an instance of a sort of case which he explicitly mentions — that in which what is commonly called 'the cause' is associated with what is commonly called 'the effect' through an intermediate series of causes and effects commonly left unmentioned, and perhaps unknown. What Hume is suggesting is this: that *even if*, in the case of the melting of lead, we *did* acquire that knowledge of its minute structure

58

which Locke thought we could not acquire, we still would not achieve *understanding* of the causal connexion in the sense which Locke supposed.

But here there is a further risk of misunderstanding. The language Locke uses makes it pretty clear that he had the notion that, if only we could discover the minute structure of matter in its various forms, then we could understand causal connexions in a quite precise sense : namely, we could say *a priori* what the properties of matter in its various forms *must be*. If only we could get at the minute mechanism, we could see, and say, that lead *must* melt when heated to about 600°, just as we can say that an equilateral triangle *must* have equal angles. Locke had the notion, that is, that a clear mechanical connexion is like a clear logical connexion : we know without experiment that an equilateral triangle is also equiangular, and *must* be equiangular ; just so, in Locke's view, if we can clearly see, say, the turning of a wheel to be mechanically connected with, say, the moving of a rod, we can say, as he puts it, 'without trial' that, if the wheel turns, the rod will move, and that in fact it *must* move. Physics meant, for Locke in the seventeenth century, mechanics ; and it was, in his view, only a practical difficulty (though indeed an insuperable one) which debarred us from establishing in physics truths every bit as demonstrative, as necessary, as mathematical theorems.

Now certainly part of what Hume meant to do was to deny this. That an equilateral triangle must be equiangular is necessary, in the precise sense that the supposition of its not being equiangular can be shown to imply a contradiction, a logical impossibility: but Hume vigorously insists that no causal truth can be necessary in this sense. We are sure in fact that a lump of lead, if heated sufficiently, will melt; but the supposition that it will not melt, but instead will burst into flame, or explode, or groan, or vanish in a puff of green smoke, is not *logically* impossible, implies no contradiction. Similarly, to come closer to Locke's notion, it seems to us certainly very evident that, if, say, two cog-wheels are engaged, then, if one turns, the other must turn in the opposite direction: but this too is not necessary as the truths of mathematics are necessary — that is, there is no contradiction in the supposition that both wheels will turn the same way, that one will not move at all, or that both will stick together in a sort of treacly amalgam.

How one body mechanically interacts with another body is after all, Hume insists, a question of empirical fact, and not, as a mathematical truth is, a question of logic: hence, a proposition founded on mechanical connexions cannot be *necessary* in the sense that the truths of mathematics are necessary. And in general, nothing that happens in the world can be connected, in this sense, *necessarily* with anything else that happens in the world; for it is never self-contradictory to suppose those conjunctions not to hold that, as a matter of fact, do hold. This thesis of Hume's is sometimes reduced to the formula that empirical propositions cannot be logically necessary: and this — being a truism, though doubtless not a trivial one — has been very widely accepted. And rightly so.

But is this, in fact, all that Hume is saying? I think not. I think it is clear that he wishes to say, not only that no causal connexion is, strictly, a necessary connexion, but also that no particular kind of causal connexion is, by contrast with any other actual or imaginable kind, specially *intelligible* or *understandable*. Even if, that is, Locke had not made the mistake of supposing that a mechanical connexion was specifically like a logical connexion, Hume would still, I think, have dissented from Locke's opinions — on the ground that those minute inner mechanisms of matter which Locke hankered to know about are not really, as Locke fancied, intelligible or understandable, in any sense in which other, more grossly observable causal regularities are not. One might put it like this: there is never, Hume says, any reason why a particular effect B should be conjoined with a particular cause A, or vice versa: so far as reason goes, as he puts it, 'anything can be the cause of anything': what actually causes what is always a matter of mere brute fact, and we deceive ourselves if we think some causal connexions to be *understandable*, in a way that other actual or possible connexions are not, or would not be.

Now this, surely, does not look like a truism. Far from it, in fact; it surely looks just untrue. Suppose, for instance, that somebody were to allege that children born on the 3rd of April when the moon is full always show, later, an unusual talent for mathematics; and suppose further that, to our surprise no doubt, extensive investigation seems to show this allegation to be true. The phenomena in question are, it appears, conjoined. Someone then says: 'Evidently, being born on the 3rd of April when the moon is full causes the development of an unusual talent for mathematics'. Would we agree with this, or even seriously consider it? No, surely we would not. This is a mere coincidence, we should say: there isn't any causal connexion. For after all, how *could* there be? How could being born on a certain date with the moon in a certain phase affect in any way, or have anything to do with, one's talent or lack of talent for mathematics? How could these two things be causally connected?

Again, if on some Thursday morning my car will not start, why do I consider, for instance, as likely to be causally relevant the fact that the preceding night was very cold and damp? Why don't I say 'Perhaps it won't start because it's Thursday?' Because surely I believe that cold and damp conditions *could* be the cause of a car not starting, but that its happening to be Thursday could not be. In general, the cause of my car not starting could not be just anything; it could not be, for instance, the mere fact that I am in a hurry, even though I may be tempted to say this in superstitious moments.

Is Hume simply mistaken, then? Is 'Anything can be the cause of anything' just one of those arresting philosophical dicta which a little reflection shows to be (alas) not true? I think we must not be too hasty in saying so. For what do I mean when I say that it being Thursday couldn't be the cause of my car's failure to start? Do I really mean anything more, Hume might ask, than that I am quite certain it isn't? But to be quite certain that something isn't so does not, strictly speaking, entitle one to say that it *couldn't* be.

Well, yes; but perhaps, in saying 'It couldn't be', I do mean something more than merely to express my conviction that it isn't: I suggest, perhaps, that its being Thursday is quite the wrong *kind of thing*, or kind of fact, to be considered as a possible cause of a car not starting — that kind of fact is just plainly not connected with the behaviour of cars, whereas cold and damp as plainly are. Put otherwise: one can understand that cold and damp might cause a car not to start, but one cannot even begin to understand the idea that it being Thursday could have that effect.

But now we must ask *why* we find the one idea understandable, and the other not. Is it not, Hume might suggest, just that the one is familiar to us, and the other isn't? Suppose it were the case — as of course, conceivably, it could have been the case — that no petrol engine would ever start on a Thursday, and this dismal fact had been familiarly known to us from our earliest years: should we then have found it unintelligible? Should we not, having thoughtlessly tried to start the car and failed, have said 'Oh, of course, it's Thursday', and have accepted that as a perfectly adequate explanation? But if so, then it being Thursday *could* be — could, if things had happened to be otherwise than they are, have been accepted as — the cause of my car's failure to start. And so, *mutatis mutandis*, could anything else.

Now, I think there is a good deal in this. It is true, I think, that what we very familiarly know, or even believe wrongly, to be the case usually does not puzzle us, seems not to call for any further explanation, seems quite understandable ; and that sometimes we think that something couldn't be true, for no better reason than that the idea of its truth is an unfamiliar one. However, this is not the whole story. For it is an important further fact, which Hume seems wholly to neglect, that our particular causal beliefs are not completely independent of one another, but fit together, and so support each other, in a systematic way. The idea that cold and damp conditions during the night might cause a car not to start on the following morning fits in, after all, not only with what we familiarly know about cars, but also with what we know in general about electricity and the combustion of vapours : there is, behind this particular phenomenon, a vast amount of highly systematised knowledge, comprehending an immense class of other phenomena as well, in terms of which this particular case can be satisfactorily explained. By contrast, the suggested connexion between the car not starting and it being Thursday is helplessly out on a limb, all on its own : even if the fact itself were familiar, it would still fit in with nothing else that we know about anything ; and it is, in that plain sense, unintelligible.

No doubt Hume would say, though, that in saying this we don't evade his point. It is, he says, a matter of mere brute fact that A causes B : A *could* have caused, and B have been caused by, anything. Now we have just urged against this that the fact that A causes B doesn't stand alone : in most cases at any rate, such a particular causal connexion can be seen to fit in with a more or less vast, and more or less extensive, *system* of knowledge — for instance with the laws of physics and chemistry — a system, furthermore, which quite definitely excludes a vast range of other imaginable possibilities. Similarly, certain hypotheses about possible causes can be seen to 'make sense' in the light of our systematic knowledge, while others, though not logically impossible, will not be taken seriously because they do not 'make sense'. But is it not, Hume would now ask, still a brute fact that this whole system of knowledge — for instance the laws of physics and chemistry — is what it is? We find out, or try to, that this is how the world in general goes; but we don't find out that it has to, we can offer no reason why the physical laws should hold that do hold. So nothing in the end is more 'intelligible' than anything else: in the end we are still confronted with a bare fact, and can look no further.

Well, I think there is something right in this, and something wrong. What is right is Hume's realisation that explanation and understanding must stop somewhere: we cannot always cite some further fact as explaining why what is the case should be the case: we must come, in the end, to what just is the case, and leave it at that. But two things are wrong. First, it is wrong to suggest, as I think Hume does, that we can tell in advance where the terminus is — at what point it is idle to look for any further explanation. And second, that the physical, causal basis of the world in general as it is, if a brute fact at all, is a pretty curious kind of brute fact; for if it were not as it is, presumably the world would be entirely different — perhaps unimaginably different ; and it is usually taken to be the mark of a bare, brute fact that we can quite well imagine how things would have been, if it had not been so. But this, or very nearly this, is what Kant was provoked by Hume to insist upon : and thus, as so often in philosophy, we end at the beginning of another long story.

6

HUME ON MORAL JUDGEMENT

Some philosophers talk about morality in an elevated tone; and they seem to be entirely sincere, finding virtue a sublime and noble subject, the pursuit of virtue an inspiring life's work. So it is, for instance, with Kant, who writes in one place about the moral law within and the starry heavens above filling the mind with ever increasing awe and admiration, the oftener and more steadily we reflect on them. It came quite naturally to Kant, as it did to Rousseau, to talk about the sublimity of our nature in its higher aspect, and of *reverence* for the moral law. 'Duty!' he says. 'Sublime and mighty name.' But Hume speaks with a very different voice.

And as every quality which is useful or agreeable to ourselves or others is, in common life, allowed to be a part of personal merit; so no other will ever be received, where men judge of things by their natural, unprejudiced reason, without the delusive glosses of superstition and false religion. Celibacy, fasting, penance, mortification, self-denial, humility, silence, solitude, and the whole train of monkish virtues; for what reason are they everywhere rejected by men of sense, but because they serve to no manner of purpose; neither advance a man's fortune in the world, nor render him a more valuable member of society; neither qualify him for entertainment of company, nor increase his power of self-enjoyment? We observe, on the contrary, that they cross all these desirable ends; stupify the understanding and harden the heart, obscure the fancy and sour the temper. We justly, therefore, transfer them to the opposite column, and place them in the catalogue of vices; nor has any superstition force enough among men of the world, to pervert entirely these natural sentiments. A gloomy, hair-brained enthusiast, after his death, may have a place in the calendar; but will scarcely ever be admitted, when alive, into intimacy and society, except by those who are as delirious and dismal as himself.

Where Kant, or Rousseau, close to Hume in time, but at a great distance in mental space, saw virtue as inspiring, Hume found it useful and agreeable, fitting a man for business and society. Indeed he actually identified a sense of virtue with a pleasing sentiment of approbation, which, he thought, men find within themselves on the contemplation of certain actions and qualities of mind. He defines virtue to be 'whatever mental action or quality gives to a spectator the pleasing sentiment of approbation; and vice the contrary'. Moreover, enquiring into the common characteristics of those actions or qualities which have this pleasant effect upon the spectator, he decides that they are all agreeable, or useful, to ourselves or other men. So a sense of virtue is itself a kind of pleasure, and this pleasure arises on the contemplation of what is useful or agreeable to mankind.

Hume's account of the common characteristics of the qualities called virtues is, it must be said, bad. It leads him to class with such things as honesty, justice, benevolence, and courage, not only cleanliness, which 'naturally renders us agreeable to others, and is a very considerable source of love and affection', but also such things as wit and eloquence. One does not find in Hume an account of the difference between skills or talents and virtues and he even says that there is no reason to consider virtue as something distinct. I suppose it is partly due to Hume's influence that this important topic, which was splendidly treated by Aristotle and Aquinas, is hardly discussed by modern moral philosophers.

But there is a much more serious charge to be laid at Hume's door. Even supposing that he had been right in saying that the things which we call virtues are the qualities useful and agreeable to ourselves and others — if these were their common characteristics — Hume's account of the *status* of the proposition 'virtues are qualities useful or agreeable, etc.' might still be attacked. For he seems to think that we find out *by observation* that these are the qualities which happen to arouse in a spectator the pleasing sentiment of approbation called the sense of virtue. We find that, as a matter of fact, people do feel the peculiar sentiment of approbation when they contemplate just these actions and qualities : but it might have been otherwise. He speaks as if we first identify the special sentiment of approbation, moral approval, and then look around to see what can be said about the things that arouse this feeling in us, thus implying that there is no difficulty in discovering that people *are* feeling approval before it is known what beliefs they hold about the things in question. Mr. Gardiner pointed out in his essay [1]

[1] p. 7.

that Hume held a similar theory about the identifi-
cation of the internal sensation of pride, and objected
that one could not really say that it was pride that
someone was feeling unless he had the right thoughts
about the thing of which he was supposed to feel
proud. (He must, I suppose, see it as something
like an achievement, and as in some way related to
himself.) A feeling of pride is not identified like a
tickle, but requires a special kind of thought about
the thing of which one feels proud. Now I should say,
though I do not know whether Mr. Gardiner would,
that it is just as bad to try to identify a feeling as a feeling of approval, whether moral approval or any other,
without its particular objects as it is to try to identify
pride without talking about the only kinds of things
about which one can *logically* feel proud. (I do not
mean, of course, that one would be illogical in feeling
pride towards something which one did not believe to
be in some way splendid and in some way one's own,
but that the concept of pride does not allow us to talk
like that.) Similarly for the concept of approval,
though the reader will kindly excuse me from giving
an account of what exactly a man must believe of those
things of which he can logically approve. Anyone
who doubts this point about approval should ask what
it would be to have *this* feeling when contemplating
an object one did not see as useful, beautiful, efficient
or anything like that. Does it make sense to suppose
that one might wake up one morning feeling approval
of something believed to be an ordinary, unnecessary,
unbeautiful speck of dust? Hume was, I think, making
a mistake when he tried to explain what it meant
to say that an action or quality was virtuous in

terms of a special feeling ; for the explanation of the thought comes into the description of the feeling, not the other way round.

Now this theory of Hume's about moral sentiment commits him to a subjectivist theory of ethics. He could not consistently maintain both that a man calls qualities virtues when he happens to feel towards them this peculiar sentiment, and that statements about virtue and vice are objective. For if they were objective, like ordinary statements of fact, there would have to be some method of deciding, in case of disagreement, whether one man's opinion or another's was correct — as the opinion that the earth is flat can be shown to be mistaken by a voyage round the globe. But since Hume has denied all logical connexions — all connexions of meaning — between moral approval and the objects of moral approval, and would have to allow anyone to assert any kinds of actions he chose to be virtuous on the strength of the supposed feeling of approbation, it follows that no one could get at an opponent who professed weird 'moral views'. And Hume himself, though he sometimes modifies his theory and talks about the sentiments of the majority, in most places accepts this subjectivism with ease, and even with relish.

Take any action allowed to be vicious : Wilful murder for instance. Examine it in all lights, and see if you can find that matter of fact, or real existence, which you call *vice*. In whichever way you take it, you find only certain passions, motives, volitions and thoughts. There is no other matter of fact in the case. The vice entirely escapes you, as long as you consider the object.

You can never find it, till you turn your reflexion into your own breast, and find a sentiment of disapprobation, which arises in you, towards this action. Here is a matter of fact; but 'tis the object of feeling, not of reason. It lies in yourself, not in the object.

Such a theory does not look at all plausible. We are not inclined to think that when a man says that an action is virtuous, or vicious, he is talking about his own feelings rather than a quality which he must show really to belong to what is done. It seems strange to suggest that he does not have to bring forward any special *fact about the action* in order to maintain what he says. So, of course, what one wants to know is why Hume adopted this strange theory: what drove him to say that the virtuousness of an action could not be a plain provable matter of fact. Sometimes, indeed, he suggests that one simply cannot find any such fact, but since he himself claims that all the things called virtues are qualities agreeable or useful to mankind why should he not say that it is in this that their virtuousness *consists*? Why does he have to bring in his feeling of approbation, and by making this the essential part of moral judgement anchor statements about virtue to the sentiments of the observer and not to the facts?

Hume would reply that one must distinguish a judgement about morality from the whole class of what he calls 'conclusions of reason' — that is, ordinary provable propositions about what is the case. For, he says, no such factual proposition could ever have a necessary connexion with the will of the man who accepted it, while it is an essential fact about a moral judgement that it does have this practical force.

'Morals excite passions, and produce or prevent actions. Reason of itself is utterly impotent in this particular. The rules of morality, therefore, are not conclusions of our reason.' Hume, who is not usually repetitious, says this kind of thing over and over again. 'As long as it is allowed, that reason has no influence on our passions and actions, 'tis in vain to pretend, that morality is discover'd only by a deduction of reason.' 'Reason is wholly inactive and can never be the source of so active a principle as conscience, or a sense of morals.'

What does Hume mean when he says that reason is wholly inactive? He argues that whenever a man is led by a judgement of reason to some action it is not reason *alone* which impels him, but reason with the co-operation of desire. Reason can tell us, for instance, that a certain action will have a particular effect, or, again, that a certain object exists within our reach; but if the effect is indifferent to us, the thing not wanted, the discovery of fact which Hume calls 'a conclusion of reason' will make no difference to what we do. And so, he says, reason alone is 'perfectly inert'; it may of course influence actions, but only when we happen to have certain desires. Thus conclusions of reason have a merely contingent connexion with action, whereas the propositions of morality are necessarily practical, going beyond the 'calm and indolent judgements of the understanding'. Between these calm and indolent judgements and the assertion that something should be done there is, Hume thinks, the famous gap between *is* and *ought*.

I cannot forbear adding to these reasonings an observation, which may, perhaps, be found of some importance. In every system of morality, which I have hitherto met with, I have always remarked, that the author proceeds for some time in the ordinary way of reasoning, and establishes the being of a God, or makes observations concerning human affairs; when of a sudden I am surpriz'd to find, that instead of the usual copulations of propositions, *is*, and *is not*, I meet with no proposition that is not connected with an *ought* or an *ought not*. This change is imperceptible; but is, however, of the last consequence. For as this *ought*, or *ought not* expresses some new relation or affirmation, 'tis necessary that it shou'd be observed and explain'd; and at the same time a reason should be given, for what seems altogether inconceivable, how this new relation can be a deduction from others, which are entirely different from it.

Hume thought that he himself had hit on the perfect solution to the problem. The new element in a proposition about virtue was the reference to a special sentiment of approbation: nothing new in the object, but something in ourselves. At a blow he seemed to have put an end to the hunt for mysterious extra properties, and also to have shown the necessary connexion between morality and the will. For the moral sentiment, the special feeling which we call approbation, was a pleasurable sentiment, by which we were inclined towards those actions whose contemplation gave rise to it. 'To know virtue is to love it.' This, Hume might have said, is a logical truth.

This extraordinary interesting theory has been

a great influence in contemporary ethics. Many
modern moral philosophers have taken up Hume's
argument and, starting from his premise about the
necessarily practical nature of morality, assert his
conclusion about the gap between *is* and *ought*.
Indeed they often make the connexion between the
propositions of morality even closer than he did,
suggesting that an actual rule of conduct rather than
a mere sentiment is required for moral judgement.
'To know virtue is to be prepared to follow it' is
what they might say. And like Hume, having
anchored moral judgement to the will of the judger,
they have cut it loose from the world.

Such theories are, I believe, wrong, and the
mistake can be traced back to the interpretation of
the crucial premise : morality is necessarily practical.
It is not that this is false, but that one may easily
insist on too close a connexion between moral judgement and the will. I do not know quite what sense
ought to be given to the proposition that morality is
necessarily practical, but two things at least can be
said. In the first place we take it as part of the
meaning of what we call 'moral terms' that they
are in general used for teaching particular kinds of
conduct; though nothing follows about what any
particular individual who uses the terms must feel
or do. Secondly, since moral virtues are qualities
necessary if men are to get on well in a world in
which they are frightened, tempted by pleasure and
liable to hurt rather than help each other, they need
virtues as they need health or strength or the ability
to make common plans. This general connexion
between such things as courage, temperance, and

justice and human good is quite enough to explain why people are often influenced by considerations of morality. They are not *necessarily* influenced, as Hume must have known; but they are concerned to teach and practise virtue in so far as they have taken this thought for their own and the common good. It is, therefore, unnecessary to posit a special sentiment to explain why observations about virtue have an influence on the will, and the *raison d'être* of Hume's subjectivist theory of ethics disappears.

7

HUME ON RELIGION

Hume died on 25 August 1776, and his burial took place four days later. In the words of his biographer, E. C. Mossner: 'A large crowd had gathered in St. David Street to watch the coffin being carried out. One of the crowd was overheard to remark, "Ah, he was an Atheist." To which a companion returned: "No matter, he was an *honest* man."'

Both statements, with the slightest of qualifications, seem to have been true. The qualification is to the first statement; if 'atheist', is taken to imply, as it often is today, 'dogmatic atheist', one who is prepared to assert with certainty that no sort of God or religious principle exists, this Hume was not. However, he fell not very far short of it, and was certainly an atheist by, say, Christian standards: about the non-existence of the Christian God, it seems clear that he felt no doubts. But there was some dimension of religious belief, in some pretty tenuous sense, about which he seems to have remained in a sceptical or agnostic position; and one problem in interpreting Hume on religion is to determine exactly how much or how little he was prepared to regard even as a matter of doubt.

The problem arises in part from the manner in which Hume approaches the subject — in the blend of irony and caution with which he writes about it.

The caution was motivated by the religious temper of the times. Even in the liberal-minded Edinburgh of the 1750s and after, there were still certain conventions about the way in which religion, and in particular, of course, Christianity, could properly be discussed, and it was incumbent on those expressing doubts to cover their attacks with some semblance of conformity. Indeed, Hume was persuaded by his friends that his *Dialogues concerning Natural Religion* — which is his greatest work on religion — could not be prudently published in his lifetime at all; and it is interesting to find him in the last few weeks of his life anxiously making dispositions to ensure that it would in fact be published after his death. In this climate, the irony that was natural to Hume's temper was of good service in assisting the demands of caution. He employs, as Kemp Smith has pointed out in his invaluable edition of the *Dialogues*, much the same methods of covering his tracks as did the French sceptic Bayle, from whom Hume learnt a lot. One such method was to claim that one was criticising not Christianity, but superstitious perversions of it; another was to claim that in destroying pretensions to rational argument in support of religious doctrines, one was only making way for Faith, on which they should properly rest. Kant, of course, who was much influenced by Hume's destructive arguments, was later to claim that this was what he was doing — 'removing Reason to make room for Faith'. The difference is that he meant it, and Hume and Bayle did not.

The irony, however, does not operate only in

the direction of caution. For just as in the *Treatise*, Hume cannot resist expressing himself in a manner designed to upset his conventional readers. It is these two, opposite, uses of irony, I think, one in the direction of prudence and one against it, that have enabled many interpreters in the past to suppose that Hume had more positive religious belief than in fact he did. For it all depends on which side of the irony you take the more seriously.

The central case of these doubts is his *Dialogues concerning Natural Religion*. This dialogue has three speakers : Demea, an orthodox Christian believer of traditional views, who is prepared to advance an *a priori* argument for the existence of God ; Cleanthes, a more moderate believer, who rests his case on the Argument from Design ; and Philo, a sceptic who seeks to subvert the force of both the arguments, and in particular devotes his efforts to refuting the Argument from Design, with which most of the work is concerned. The conversation between these persons is narrated, moreover, by a speaker who says that he agrees with Cleanthes, the moderate believer. This structure has in the past led defenders of Hume's orthodoxy to suppose that Hume himself rejected Philo's sceptical arguments : in much the same way, perhaps, as in the *Treatise*, philosophical doubts about the existence of the material world are rejected as strained and unnatural, as trying to run against the unavoidable force of natural belief. On this interpretation, it is in the person of Philo that Hume speaks ironically, to shock, and in the persons of Cleanthes and the narrator, the moderate orthodox, that he speaks directly.

But this interpretation, it would now generally be agreed, is wrong : the irony is the other way round. Kemp Smith has shown that it is the sceptical views of Philo that most closely express Hume's own. Indeed, we know from his life that he rejected Christian doctrines. He was brought up in a Calvinist household — not the most narrow and repressive of such households as could be found in Scotland in those times, but rigorous enough. In his late 'teens he worked his way out of these beliefs, and — he explicitly states in a letter — never returned to them, nor to any form of Christianity. When he was dying, indeed, he calmly reaffirmed his disbelief in orthodoxy and the after-life to Boswell, who egregiously took the occasion to exhort him to reconsider his views. In private correspondence, he uses the word 'Christian' as a mild term of abuse : he said of Rousseau, when he had too late discovered what Rousseau was like, 'he has a hankering after the Bible, and is indeed little better than a Christian in a way of his own' ; and in 1765 he described the English as 'relapsing fast into the deepest stupidity, Christianity and ignorance'. Particularly in the earlier years of his adult life, he was strongly anti-clerical, even though later he became friends with various Moderate divines in Edinburgh.

Apart from these biographical evidences, it can be seen from Hume's theories that he could not have held that sceptical doubts about God's existence were in the same position as sceptical doubts about, for instance, the existence of the external world. It is of the essence of Hume's position that those latter doubts run against nature : that one *cannot* doubt

the existence of material bodies, except perhaps for
very brief periods in a very unnatural state of mind.
But he does not regard the belief in religion as in
this sense natural or inevitable at all. He does
indeed think that it has natural roots, in the sense
that a naturalistic account can be given of why people
believe in religion, and this he attempted to give
in the work called *The Natural History of Religion*.
But this is a different matter; and it is notable that
he did not believe, as did many apologists of his
own and later times, that religious belief was a
universal phenomenon among mankind.

While it is certain that Hume did not regard
religious belief as natural, in his special sense of that
term — that is, as something which human nature,
by its very constitution, must embrace — there are
certain obscurities in his account of it. Here it is
best, perhaps, to look first at the theory of *The
Natural History of Religion*. His basic thesis in this
work is that polytheism is an earlier belief than
monotheism, the latter arising only by a later process.
The source of the original polytheism he locates in
men's incomprehension and fear of various circumstances that affect them : because of the unknown
and hidden causes of such things as droughts, tem-
pests, sickness and so forth, men are primitively led
to posit a collection of independent personal agencies
to account for these things. In advancing this view
that polytheism was primary, Hume is implicitly
criticising thinkers of a Deist temper, as well as
some of the orthodox, who supposed that primitive
man had already an apprehension of the universe
as designed and created by a single designer. On

the contrary, this he supposes to be a belief that arises afterwards; roughly, he thinks that one god gets advanced over the others because of emulation in praising and admiring him; and that when he is established as *the* God, men find reasons, such as the Argument from Design, to prove his existence.

Not only does Hume think that polytheism is primary over monotheism; he also believes — or claims to believe — that it is superior. He has two reasons in particular for this. First, polytheism is more tolerant: the Greeks and Romans, for instance, were always prepared to assimilate other people's gods. Monotheism, on the other hand, by its very nature tends to intolerance and absolutism. From this greater tolerance of polytheism, Hume is disposed to infer, in general, its greater benevolence; but since he himself mentions the polytheistic Mexicans for the barbarism of their practices, this seems hardly a valid inference. The second reason for the superiority of polytheism is that it does less violence to reason. This is not because it is more reasonable; on the contrary, it is a complete muddle of inconsistent myths and absurd superstitions. The point is that just because it is so, it does not admit of any serious attempt to rationalise it. The trouble with monotheism is that it encourages men to rationalise religion, to try to make a philosophical and theological system out of it, and *so long as the religion preserves its dogmas*, this can only lead to doing violence to reason itself; one is led into an endless path of pseudo-reasoning, which is worse, because more corrupting and dishonest, than the primitive confusions of polytheism.

Hume is not, of course, recommending polytheism ; he thinks that no reasonable and civilised
man would dream of accepting it. Here we meet
a distinction important to Hume's account of
religion ; a fairly commonplace eighteenth-century
distinction between the vulgar and the sophisticated.
The vulgar perhaps need a religion : if so, polytheism
may well be better, as doing less harm. The sophisticated may well do without one : the trouble is
that the religion they may be tempted to embrace
may be even worse than the primitive one. Here
also, and in some ways parallel, is a distinction that
Hume makes between superstition and fanaticism.
By the first he means an assemblage of mythical
beliefs, such as those of polytheism, which may do
little harm ; by the latter, the proselytising zealotry
of religions such as Christianity, which he thinks is
straightforwardly pernicious.

Hume has been criticised for his one-sided selec-
tion of the phenomena of religion. He emphasises
over and over again the power of religion to lead
men into persecution, unreason, and hatred ; he
says little, it has been pointed out, on the power of
religion to induce love, charity or steadfastness.
This is indeed true. But here we have to remember
Hume's moral theory, by which men have a natural
tendency to sympathy and benevolence. If then,
religious men act benevolently, they do not so act
because of religion — they so act because they are
men. It is persecution and hatred that need the
explanation, and religion only too often provides it.
Now this is obviously a very limited and inadequate
account of the effects of religious belief — just as,

we may add, the story about men's fears of the unknown is an inadequate account of its origins. In both cases, the limitations lie in the general body of Hume's philosophy : in the one case, in his moral psychology, in the other, in a limited empiricist theory about the origins of belief. Hume, like Bertrand Russell in our own time, is too amiable and optimistic a man really to understand religion.

I have mentioned Hume's distinction between the attitudes of the vulgar and of the sophisticated to religion ; and I have pointed out that in his view one form of sophisticated religion was worse than the vulgar superstitious sort. Is there then no way in which sophisticated monotheism is superior to other religious beliefs ? It would seem from the previous account that there was not. Yet it does seem that there is one sense in which sophisticated monotheism may be nearer in Hume's view to *something* which it would be perverse or unwise to deny : he indeed says that the excesses of fanatical monotheism illustrate the maxim, *corruptio optimi pessima*, the worst of things is the corruption of the best. What, then, is the best ? What is this something that may be left over when the bad accretions of religion are stripped away ?

To find this, we must look at the *Dialogues concerning Natural Religion* ; and particularly, granted the previous claim that the speeches of Philo represent Hume, at those speeches. Now Sir Leslie Stephen said that the *Dialogues* was the first sustained philosophical criticism of the Argument from Design. I do not know for certain whether this is true ; what is certain is that, in a slightly different sense, it is the last — after it there did not need to be another. Although the Argument from Design lingered on through the nineteenth century, and even to the present time, Hume undermined it in a through-going and definitive manner. The essence of the Argument, as used in Natural Theology — that is, as an argument actually to prove the existence of the Christian God — is that it is a type of empirical argument, an argument from effect to cause. Hume's objections add up to saying that as such an argument, it does not work. For first, in positing a cause for an observed effect, one is not justified in positing more in the cause than is strictly necessary to produce the effect, and this the Argument does, by positing an infinite, omniscient, etc. being as the cause of what may well be, for all we know, a finite world. Again, the argument assumes that the only cause of organisation, such as we see in the world about us, can be intelligence. But this is quite gratuitous; in our experience we see organisation proceeding from many principles other than intelligence, as for instance, animals from animals and plants from plants; why should we not as well assume the creator of the world to have been some animal or vegetable, rather than a mind? Indeed, the supposition of mind as the first cause is particularly gratuitous, since on every hand we see mind proceeding from matter, but not matter from mind. More generally, there is a fundamental fault in the argument. It is an argument from analogy; but arguments from analogy depend upon repeated occurrences of the instances to which they apply. But in this special case, this condition cannot be satisfied: we only have one world to argue about. Hence any analogy employed must be extremely weak, if it has any strength at all. All this is consistent with Hume's views on empirical inference, and they are certainly appropriate, for it was in a special application of empirical inference that the argument was supposed to have its strength.

There is a further point. The Argument from Design was supposed to show not merely the existence of a designer, but his benevolence. Here Hume thought that the evidence was not merely too weak to bear the conclusion, but, in some respects, downright opposed to it. While granting the beauty and fitness of final causes in nature, which move our thoughts towards a designer, Philo adds: 'But there is no view of human life or of the condition of mankind, from which without the greatest violence, we can infer the moral attributes, or learn that infinite benevolence, conjoined with infinite power and infinite wisdom, which we must discover by the eyes of faith alone'. And when Cleanthes replies that no doubt what seems inconvenient and terrible in human life seems so only because of our ignorance of some Divine plan, Philo replies with one of Hume's most important observations in this connexion: that while such considerations might serve to *reconcile* the state of man's life with Divine benevolence, if the latter were independently proved, they certainly cannot assist us to *prove* this benevolence from the state of man's life.

Apart from this further application of the criticism of the analogical argument, Hume has in any case an *a priori* reason for disbelieving in God's moral attributes. On his moral theory, moral attributes are derived from human nature, and only make sense in relation to it — our ideas of moral goodness are necessarily ideas of human goodness, and could not conceivably be applied to a non-human, infinite being. Indeed, in a letter to Francis Hutcheson, with whose moral theory his own had much in common, he criticises him for inconsistency in supposing that moral attributes could be applied to the Deity.

After all this, little seems to be left of the Argument from Design, or indeed of the Christian conception of God. Hume indeed thinks that the very idea of praying to God, or in the ordinary sense, worshipping him, must be inappropriate, for not only does it involve regarding God as like a man, but as like a not very admirable type of man : 'To know god', he makes Philo say, 'is to worship him. All other worship is indeed absurd, superstitious and even impious.' But now, what God? Well, Hume throughout the *Dialogues* is certainly impressed by the existence of the regulated final causes of nature ; and he does sum up Philo's position by allowing him to assent to the 'somewhat ambiguous, at least undefined proposition, that the cause or causes of order in the universe probably bear some remote analogy to human intelligence'. This is the most that he thinks a reasonable man can assent to ; and what is certain is that anything which might be called religion based on this proposition should have no prayer, no worship, no institutions, and no effect on moral conduct. The vague shadow of a possible religious belief is so remote that it could have no effect.

Hume was a sceptic, not a materialist. This was one reason why he objected, as he did, to the dogmatic tone of the French *philosophes*. For him, the ultimate causes of things remained necessarily mysterious; we know enough, he thought, to know that most things said about God must be false and inappropriate, and we can see further that attempts to argue to his existence must be useless. But we do not know what the ultimate origin of anything is, and cannot — we do not know enough to — exclude the possibility that something rather like an intelligence might — just conceivably — have something to do with it. One suspects that he had another reason for his objections to the *philosophes*, which was that they got too excited about the non-existence of God. He smelt the odour of a negative fanaticism, and any fanaticism, for Hume, was as bad as any other. Consistently with his philosophy, it would be the human effects of unbelief, as of belief, that would concern him most.

8

HUME AS A HISTORIAN

DAVID HUME was the greatest of British philosophers. He was also an important figure
in the development of the social sciences.
We do not often think of him as a historian. Yet
when he died, in 1776, he was better known as a
historian than as a philosopher. He was the first,
and for long the most famous, of the so-called 'philosophical historians' in Britain, of whom the second
was William Robertson, now unjustly neglected,
and the third Edward Gibbon. We now recognise
Gibbon as by far the greatest; but Gibbon himself,
all his life, bowed modestly before the other two.
In his early days they were the models whom he
aspired to imitate; when his first volume was published it was their praise which most delighted him;
and even at the height of his fame it never occurred
to him to challenge their supremacy. 'I have never
presumed', he wrote, 'to accept a place in the trium-
virate of British historians.' There can be no question of Gibbon's genuine humility in the presence
of 'the calm philosophy, the careless inimitable
beauties' of 'the Tacitus of Scotland', David
Hume.

Yet Hume, unlike Gibbon, became a historian
almost by accident. In 1752, after a great electoral
battle which he has described in one of his most

entertaining letters, he was elected Librarian of the Advocates' Library in Edinburgh, and there, sitting among those 30,000 volumes, he suddenly saw his opportunity. 'You know', he wrote to a friend, 'that there is no post of honour in the English Parnassus more vacant than that of History. Style, judgement, impartiality — everything is wanting to our historians'; and so he decided to fill the vacant throne. He would write the history of England. No sooner had he decided than he set to work. Beginning at 1603, his pen moved briskly forward; and as he wrote he became entranced with the subject. 'The more I advance in my undertaking', he wrote, 'the more I am convinced that the History of England has never yet been written, not only for style, which is notorious to all the world, but also for matter; such is the ignorance and partiality of our historians. Rapin, whom I had an esteem for, is totally despicable. . . .' Rapin — a French Huguenot who had been taken up by Dutch William, lived in Germany, and wrote in French — was the fashionable historian of the time; he was the official historian of his triumphant patrons, the English Whigs.

For in the 1750s the whigs still had it all their own way. As Hume himself wrote, 'for a course of near seventy years, almost without interruption' they had 'enjoyed the whole authority of the government, and no honours nor offices could be obtained but by their countenance and protection'. This whig victory, he admitted, had been 'advantageous to the state'; but unfortunately the whigs had not been content with political triumph: they had 'assumed a right to impose upon the public their account of all particular transactions, and to represent the other party [*i.e.* the tories] as governed entirely by the lowest and most vulgar prejudices'. In fact the whigs had established the doctrine that the English constitution, even before 1688, was 'a regular plan of liberty', and that the whigs, and they alone, had been the faithful champions of this constitution, the devoted idealists of liberty. Hume's researches in the Advocates' Library convinced him that this doctrine was 'ridiculous', and in his first volume, which was published in 1754 and covered the reigns of James I and Charles I, he offered what he considered a juster, more 'moderate view'.

Like all historians, Hume considered himself entirely impartial. 'I may be liable to the reproach of ignorance', he wrote, 'but I am certain of escaping that of partiality.' After all, why should he be partial? He was a foreigner, a Scotsman, happily outside the factious party politics of England for which he always expressed the greatest contempt. He was also a social philosopher, with a new point of view : a point of view from which politics receded into the interstices left by social and economic laws. And in religion he was a sceptic — 'that notorious infidel', as Johnson and Boswell called him — for whom religion too receded into its social context. For all these reasons he felt himself outside and above the stale and vulgar battles of whig and tory, Church and Dissent. He was a 'philosophic historian', and having written a philosophic history of the reigns of the first two Stuart kings, he sat back and awaited the applause.

It did not come. Instead, as he afterwards wrote in his brief autobiography:

I was assailed by one cry of reproach, disapprobation and even detestation. English, Scotch and Irish, whig and tory, churchman and sectary, free-thinker and religionist, patriot and courtier united in their rage against the man who had presumed to shed a generous tear for the fate of Charles I and the earl of Stafford; and after the first ebullitions of their fury were over, what was still more mortifying, the book seemed to sink into oblivion . . . I scarcely indeed heard of one man in the three kingdoms considerable for rank or letters that could endure the book. I must only except the primate of England, Dr. Herring, and the primate of Ireland, Dr. Stone, which seem two odd exceptions. These dignified prelates separately sent me messages not to be discouraged.

In fact, says Hume, he was so discouraged that, but for the outbreak of war, he would have retired permanently to a provincial town in France, changed his name, 'and never more have returned to my native country'.

However, he persevered. In 1756 he published his next volume, covering the period from 1649 to 1689. This volume, he says, 'happened to give less displeasure to the whigs and was better received. It not only rose itself, but helped to buoy up its unfortunate brother'. Then, instead of following his original plan and coming forward to his own time, where he now despaired of gaining access to the sources, he went back and wrote two more volumes covering the Tudor dynasty, and finally another two on medieval England. By 1761 his history was complete : a history of England from Julius Caesar to William III. But the most famous, most controversial part remained the first two volumes published : the volumes covering that permanent historical minefield, the seventeenth century.

Of the controversy aroused by Hume's history I shall say something further. But first of all let me make a general point. Neither Hume nor any of the 'philosophical historians' of the eighteenth century wrote vivid history. They did not seek, as their successors after the Romantic movement did, to plunge back, bodily and mentally, into the past. Archaic language, local colour — these devices for bringing the reader himself into the scenes of history never occurred to them. They sat in Edinburgh, or London, or Lausanne and wrote about remote, unvisited countries and distant, disagreeable centuries in the cool style of the eighteenth century. The idea that they should become part of the past, wear its clothes, sink into its conventions, sympathise with its bigotries, would have shocked them. A rational man, living in 'the full light and freedom of the eighteenth century', might look back into the Dark Ages, but only an idiot or a monk would seek to plunge back into them. History, the philosophical historians believed, was an intellectual exercise : it required a modern mind, and should be expressed in modern language. They aimed at social analysis, not description of antique costume, elegant paraphrase, not quotation of bizarre texts. No doubt this makes them less vivid than their successors, but it has its advantages. Too many of those successors plunged back only into the clothes, not the mind, of the past: and today the judicious mind of the eighteenth century often seems more modern as well as more humane than the misplaced sympathies of the nineteenth. Hume, Robertson and Gibbon are more modern than Motley or Freeman, more humane than Macaulay or Froude.

Apart from this general point, we must remember that Hume was not an Englishman, but a Scot. This was of great significance, because the coming of the Enlightenment, which he represented, was very different in Scotland and in England. In both countries, as in all Europe, the Enlightenment was largely the triumph of lay reason over clerical bigotry. But the bigots in the two countries were different. In England they were tory parsons; therefore the English Enlightenment wore 'whig' colours. In Scotland they were the ministers of the 'whigga-more' Kirk; therefore the Scottish Enlightenment was a tory movement. Hume's 'toryism' is an obvious result of this fact. He had himself had plenty of trouble from the bigots of the Kirk, and he could never accept the easy English orthodoxy that men who opposed the Stuarts, or were oppressed by them, were thereby necessarily friends of liberty or truth.

Perhaps I may illustrate these points by a few quotations. In the seventeenth century, during the Puritan Revolution, the Scots thought they would only be safe if they could force their own church system on the more advanced society of England; and they made a determined effort to do so. They demanded it in treaties, made it the condition of their support, and sent a pack of dogmatising clergymen to London as propagandists. A modern historian would no doubt suspend his own judgement and quote the tedious sermons, thus giving temporal colour. Hume does neither. 'Never', he says firmly, 'did refined Athens so exult in diffusing the sciences and liberal arts over a savage world, never did generous Rome so please herself in the view of law and order established by her victorious arms, as the Scotch now rejoiced in communicating their barbarous zeal and theological fervour to the neighbouring nations.' And when he describes the London sermons of these missionaries, he is no less summary. Neither the preachers nor their enthusiastic audience obtain much sympathy :

Those who were so happy as to find access early in the morning kept their places the whole day. Those who were excluded clung to the doors or windows, in the hope of catching at least some distant murmur or broken phrases of the holy rhetoric. All the eloquence of parliament, now well refined from pedantry, animated with the spirit of liberty, and employed in such important interests, was not attended to with such insatiable avidity as were these lectures, delivered with ridiculous cant and a provincial accent, full of barbarism and ignorance.

Later in the seventeenth century, just before the Glorious Revolution in England, the Marquis of Argyle tried to raise a whig revolt against the Stuart despotism in Scotland. To the English whig historians, this was a glorious blow for freedom, and Argyle (who was executed) a martyr in its cause. Hume will have none of this. He knew Scotland too well. 'It was in vain', he says, 'that Argyle summoned a nation so lost to all sense of liberty, so degraded by repeated iniquities, to rise in vindication of their violated laws and privileges. The greater part of those who declared for him were his own vassals : men who, if possible, were still more sunk in slavery than the rest of the nation.' All the politics of seventeenth-century Scotland seemed to Hume barbarous; the only great man whom Scotland then produced, he thought, was Napier of Merchistoun, the inventor of logarithms.

So far, we may say, Hume is indeed objective. Looking at the past without the customary whig blinkers, and with the new social spectacles, he saw that no party, political or religious, had a monopoly of political or intellectual virtue. Historical situations were created by objective social laws, and individual human beings interpreted or failed to interpret those laws. So, in each volume of his history, he wrote a short section on social history; he periodically deduced or applied social formulae; and he treated historical characters not, like his whig predecessors (or even the greatest of his whig successors, Macaulay), as heroes or villains but as individuals to whom, within this general framework, it was easier to be just, because he sought not to take sides but to explain. He was, he thought, impartial. And indeed, in personal matters, he was impartial. His bias, if he had one, was in a different field, in the philosophy that lay behind his history and informed it throughout.

For Hume was not only a social historian who, by his freedom from whig prejudices, redressed the balance of history : he was also, in his whole social outlook, a conservative. This is very clear when we consider his treatment of religion. Basically, Hume considered that all religious doctrines were equally untrue. This being so, different religions must be judged by their social usefulness. But how is social usefulness defined? It might be defined as social challenge. If Hume had been a radical, he might well have defined it thus, and then he would have excused incidental religious fanaticism when it clearly represented such a challenge. But in fact he defined it otherwise. For him, as for Gibbon, a good Church was one which does not trouble men with too much doctrine, which forwards, or at least does not oppose, art and letters, and which, preferably, is governed by laymen : in other words, an established Church which has accepted the society around it and become settled, civilised and worldly. So we find him preferring the Renaissance Popes to the 'enraged and fanatical Reformers'. 'That delicious country where the Roman pontiff resides', he wrote, 'was the source of all modern art and refinement and diffused on its superstition an air of politeness which distinguishes it from the gross rusticity of other sects.' And in the seventeenth century we find him excusing 'the mild humane Charles' whose 'inoffensive liturgy' — *i.e.* the Anglican Prayer Book — was so unreasonably assailed by the philistine Scotch clergy. Of Archbishop Laud, the architect of that fatal policy, Hume might admit that he showed, in his narrow-minded clericalism, 'the intemperate zeal of sectary', but he adds, ''tis sufficient vindication to observe that his errors were the most excusable of all those which prevailed during that

zealous period'. Words such as these can hardly
have been welcome in Woburn or Chatsworth,
far less in Galloway or Fife; but we can see
why it was that the infidel philosopher was en-
couraged to persevere in his historical studies by
the primates of the Established Church in England
and Ireland.

The publication, in 1761, of his last volume was
not the end of Hume's *History*. Once excited by
the subject, he never gave it up. In 1763 he was
appointed secretary to the British Embassy in Paris.
Because of his literary fame, all the doors of Paris
were open to him, and they included the doors of
hitherto closed historical archives. He found his
way into the Archives of the French Foreign Office
and discovered there the secret treaty of 1681 between
Charles II and Louis XIV. He found his way into
the Scots College and discovered 'a prodigious
historical curiosity, the memoirs of King James II
in fourteen volumes, all wrote with his own hand'.
And having found the way, he opened it to others.
In particular, he told a fellow-Scotsman, Sir John
Dalrymple, where to find interesting material about
the intrigues of the virtuous whigs with the exiled
Jacobite court. This hint was soon to bear ex-
plosive fruit. In the 1770s, while Hume was
quietly going through his *History* either softening or
expunging (as he said) 'many villainous seditious
whig strokes which had crept into it' — he made a
hundred alterations to his first volume, he said,
'all invariably to the tory side' — Dalrymple
convulsed the whig establishment by publishing the
despatches of Paul Barillon, the French ambassador

to Charles II: despatches which showed that the famous whig martyrs Lord Russell and Algernon Sidney were among the secret agents or pensioners of Louis XIV.

Dalrymple's discovery, greeted by hysterical screams from the whigs, set the seal on Hume's work. From now on Rapin was forgotten. If the whigs had dominated the last seventy years, the next seventy years were dominated by Hume. His *History*, in those years of tory ascendancy, was the standard History of England; and the whigs, driven back on their citadel of Holland House, knew their enemy. It was after reading Hume that Charles James Fox began and Sir James Mackintosh completed their rival whig versions of the Glorious Revolution, in order to correct 'the false impression which that great historian's partiality might have left on the mind of his readers'. But even Fox and Mackintosh had to follow where Hume led; they used the archives which he had discovered, and they accepted, however reluctantly, the conclusions which he and Dalrymple had established. Finally the greatest of all the Holland House historians set out deliberately to break, and did break, the spell of Hume. 'Hume', wrote Macaulay, was 'an accomplished advocate' who 'without positively asserting much more than he can prove' contrived to build up, by selective emphasis, a partisan case: he, Macaulay, had 'a more just conception of history. . .'. Like Hume, Macaulay thought of himself as impartial. But even Macaulay, that marvellously accomplished advocate, who was so skilful in selective emphasis, did not seek to set up again the 'ridiculous' whig conception of the eighteenth century. That had been shattered, with philosophic elegance, by the most elegant of British philosophers, temporarily turned historian, David Hume.

THE END

PRINTED BY R. & R. CLARK, LTD., EDINBURGH